The New DEI and ERG Frontier

How You and Your Efforts Can Rise and Thrive in the New World of Constant Disruption

By Joseph Santana

Table of Contents

Foreword

Over the past decades, diversity, equity, and inclusion have become a considerable force in the corporate world. Today, there are over 20,000 books on Amazon on the topic of diversity, another 6,000 with the word "equity" in their titles, and about 9,000 that talk about inclusion. So, what's different about this book? The answer is simple. This book is the first to explore the new forces that are today calling for a reshaping of our DEI practice to meet the demands of the exponentially faster-paced and disruptive digital era we've entered.

As the CEO of an integrated health care system who wants to continue being a top decile employer and provider of health care services, this book is important to me. Our organization serves a large, diverse urban area. As much as we work to bring in more diversity of insights into the ranks of our executive team, these leaders simply do not possess all the perspectives of our stakeholders. These "blind spots" can often prevent us from seeing obstacles and opportunities coming our way. I need the insights of future-thinking DEI leaders and their resource group communities to ensure that I am not flying blindly into the unknown without considering various critical workforce and marketplace perspectives. That's why I need to have DEI professionals and business resource group community leaders who are looking out into the future and providing my executive team and me with their future insights.

As a health care executive, I can see that change is speeding up in my industry. Just look at the shrinking timeline for vaccine development. It took centuries to develop a vaccine for smallpox. It took almost three decades to develop the first Flu vaccine in more recent history. (The Spanish Flu first appeared in 1918, and the vaccine was developed in 1945). On the other hand, the COVID-19 vaccine was developed and went from the lab to market in 300 days. If you think that was fast, consider this – scientists are now working to compress that feat into 100 days or less. This speeding pace of change is not confined to the health care industry. Around the world, long-established industries in every field see equally huge and exponentially growing massive disruptions.

These rapid disruptions and changes are also speeding changes in our workforce pool and total available market demographics. New technologies are increasing the number of jobs that people from anywhere on the planet can perform. New worker-organization relationship models are replacing our employee-centric workforce models. Our workforce teams are being redistributed across a new multi-dimensional workplace. At the same time, our workforce and marketplaces are becoming increasingly diverse. These and other forces present the modern-day business leader with a treasure trove of opportunities and an equal measure of potential threats.

CEOs and other company leaders need DEI professionals and business resource group leaders equipped to help them face these new challenges and opportunities. Many DEI practices today we're built with the sole goal of assisting the organization in hiring more underrepresented people. This is a legacy from the 1960's forces that first brought these practices to corporations. In recent decades, however, savvy leaders in major organizations have realized that this narrow focus was not enough to address the challenges of the 1990s and the early decades of the 21st Century. Their DEI efforts needed to transcend these limits and operate more like a management business practice. In today's leading companies, that means DEI is a factor across every aspect of business planning, not just HR. Today's business challenges demand that DEI practices, along with all other parts of the organization, evolve from being fast-reactive to being foresightful and proactive. Many of the old, so-called best practices of that slower, more stable past will not scale to meet these current and future challenges.

Like all other business leaders, DEI professionals and resource group leaders need to become futurists. They need to look at the signals of coming change to the workforce, workplace, and marketplace through their diverse lenses and come up with potential outcomes and solutions. They also need to be structured to quickly communicate these perspectives to business leaders throughout the enterprise.

To help us address that challenge, I can think of no one better suited than the author of this book, Joseph Santana. For close to a decade of our DEI journey, Joe has been a valued partner to Froedtert Health. As a former line executive with total profit and loss responsibility for a successful three hundred employee outsourcing business where he leveraged DEI to increase revenue year over year, he brings a unique business perspective to this arena.

As you will also see in this book, Joe is a futurist whose passion and focus is leveraging DEI. His uncanny ability to see the secondary and tertiary effects of events unfolding in the present across one, five, and even ten years into the future has provided partners like my organization with a substantial competitive advantage. In this book, Joe offers readers the insights and tools he's developed over decades of practice and research.

As mentioned earlier, before entering the DEI space, Joe was a front-line business leader. As the head of outsourcing for Siemens IT outsourcing business in the Greater New York Metro Area, covering all of New York City and parts of New Jersey and Connecticut, he led a team of three hundred employees that generated more than $50 million in revenue annually. When Joe noticed an increasing number of female professionals began to enter the IT outsourcing space, he led the launch of a program that removed barriers to the development of female leaders. That gave his team a competitive advantage that produced year over year double-digit revenue growth. Shortly after installing those programs, many of the business relationships within Joe's territory went global, creating even more significant sums of revenue with an increasing marketplace footprint.

Due to those accomplishments within his business unit, Joe was tapped to lead Siemens DEI efforts across their 65,000 employee multi-business unit US operations. In a little over three years, he put in place a structure that leveraged over sixty business resource groups, increased the attraction and engagement of formally underrepresented groups, and combined the total enterprise's supplier diversity purchasing power. As a result, Siemens leapfrogged over their competition, took a small multi-million-dollar portfolio of municipal, state, city, and federal contracts, and developed them into a significant one billion dollar plus public services business.

Upon leaving the corporate arena, Joe worked with major well-known organizations to take their DEI efforts to the next level. Here is a partial list of Joe's contributions to this work:

- □ His last book, **Supercharge Your ERGs – 18 Tips to Powerup Your ERG/BRG Strategy,** has helped hundreds of thousands of new ERG/BRG leaders to put their communities on the fast track toward success.
- □ His **ERG PowerTalk** podcast makes learning freely available to more than 300,000 podcast listeners across several popular channels.
- □ His monthly, **Sharpening the Axe** sessions with members of the CDO PowerCircle provide Chief Diversity Officers with the tools they need to address emerging opportunities and threats.
- □ His annual **Future DEI Foresight Summit** helps CDOs and resource group community leaders see the signals of upcoming near and long-term change to prepare to pounce on opportunities and turn obstacles into advantages.

In summary, Joe has continued to develop the skills and abilities of DEI professionals and resource group community leaders at all levels of organizations as effective futurists and partners to their CEOs and business leadership.

Judging by the scramble to respond to the recent pandemic, many organizations, despite all the rhetoric about being flexible and responsive to change, are still moving too slow for today's pace. It's not easy to pivot and change directions when leading a large organization. As Robert Toomey, Managing Director and Associate General Counsel at SIFMA, once said, "*Turning the battleship around is a slow process.*" In that quote, Toomey goes on to say, "*. . . but management is starting to get it.*" The fact is we need to "*start getting it*" much faster. To that end, we need leaders at all levels to begin thinking like futurists. This is especially true for leaders involved in helping us marshal all our diverse resources and perspectives so that we, business leaders, can make the best decisions for our organizations.

With that in mind, I urge all my fellow CEOs and business leaders to encourage their diversity professionals and resource group community leaders to get and read this book.

Catherine A. Jacobson,
President and CEO
Froedtert Health

Preface

I once told a group of people that at least two speeches were created every time I had a keynote engagement: The speech I planned to give and the one I gave. This book has followed that pattern. The book I originally planned to write was about the need for DEI teams to prepare to continue driving value in a world where AI was increasingly making essential people and business decisions. But part of me kept thinking that this was only part of an immense challenge facing DEI leaders. This eventually led me to realize that what DEI and resource groups leaders needed is a book to prepare them for a multifaceted, high-speed, exponentially evolving world.

This book you're reading is the sum of decades of research into books and papers, hundreds of interviews, and my unquenchable passion for deciphering signals from the future. Its goal is simple. To future proof you and your practice and prepare you to grow your impact and influence in an increasingly disruptive landscape.

As a futurist, I tend to look at signals and determine possible outcomes and strategies. I am not in the business of making predictions because, as the great Yogi Berra once said, "*It's tough to make predictions, especially about the future.*" But departing from that wisdom, I will make one prediction. In the wake of the George Floyd murder, there was a massive spike in hiring for diversity-leadership jobs. My prediction is simple; as the social clamor dies down and is replaced by other concerns and the speed of disruption keeps throwing business leaders into a new daily tailspin, many of those roles will be eliminated. And along with them, some DEI leadership roles that predate the social unrest, will go by the wayside as well.

I say this with the utmost confidence based on three facts. One is the events we've seen in recent history. How often has there been a corporate feeding frenzy for DEI roles following a loss of interest after the news cycle dies down? Second, in my discussions with many CEOs, some admittedly have no clue what value their DEI efforts provide, beyond making some employees happy, and their company look good. In other words, these business leaders see the work of their DEI leader as some nice-to-have hybrid HR/PR program. The third is that with today's increasing speed of change and disruptions, companies are going to want to trim the fat to the bone. Programs and efforts seen as "nice-to-have" will get a "nice-to-have" level budget and will be the first cast overboard when the business ship feels it's in trouble. And let's face it, when you're fighting for your business life, there are two things do not seem to be a priority. One is programs that celebrate food, fun, and flags to make some of your employees feel happier. The other is paying someone to go on stage and say how nice you are as a company to produce vague soft benefits.

On the other hand, DEI efforts that help their CEOs and business leaders make better decisions that support their competitive advantage in hiring the best talent across all demographics and expanding the company's total market will be pure gold. These DEI leaders will be as indispensable as the sales teams that bring in revenue. These DEI leaders will thrive, and rightly so. These DEI leaders will create real, measurable value by adding diverse perspectives to the interpretation of future signals and creating equitable organizations where everyone can indeed be their best in an inclusive atmosphere.

We truly live at a time of upheaval and disruptions that multiply every day. But, as the great physicist, Albert Einstein once said, "In the middle of difficulty lies opportunity." I wrote this book because I believe your best days as leaders in DEI are ahead of you. You are now in a position to take your place at the table as a critical management strategy partner. I trust this book will help you prepare to meet your destiny.

CHAPTER 1

Introduction: Toto, We're Not in Kansas Anymore

"The journey of the hero is about the courage to seek the depths; the image of creative rebirth; the eternal cycle of change within us; the uncanny discovery that the seeker is the mystery which the seeker seeks to know." – ***The Hero's Journey: Joseph Campbell on His Life & Work***

In the 1939 movie, *The Wizard of Oz*, Dorothy, the character played by Judy Garland, says to her dog at one point, "Toto, I have a feeling we're not in Kansas anymore." It's a phrase that has come to mean that we have stepped outside of what is considered normal and entered an unfamiliar and perhaps uncomfortable place. Most people believe this condition of dislocation we've entered since late 2019 and early 2020, is terrible. Many can't wait for it to pass. But is this truly just a dire situation that we must hope to hunker down and survive? Is it simply a bad thing? I don't think so. I believe it could be the beginning of your hero's journey.

The term "The Hero's Journey" was coined by Joseph Campbell, a professor of Literature, at Sarah Lawrence College. Campbell discovered that all the stories about heroes throughout history followed a similar formula. In 1949, he published his finding on the common structure of all the journeys characters undertake in literature, on their path to becoming heroes in his book *The Hero with a Thousand Faces*. It's a fascinating book that exposes a simple formula that repeatedly appears in the stories of religious and secular heroes of old and modern times. Here are two examples of hero's journeys. One account is from approximately 725 BC, and the other is from a 1999 cult classic movie.

In the *Odyssey*, written by Homer, our emerging hero is Odysseus. The story begins with Odysseus at home with his wife and son. Suddenly, this ordinary life is turned upside down when Odysseus is called to fight the Trojans. At first, Odysseus doesn't want to leave his family. But with the guidance of the goddess, Athena, who disguises herself as Mentor, Odysseus goes off to war. During his journey, he battles with Polyphemus, the Cyclops, is drawn into a love affair with the witch-goddess, Circe, faces temptation by the deadly Sirens, and fights the sea monster, Scylla. He is tested at every turn. He even descends into Hades, the land of the dead, to consult the prophet Tiresias. Odysseus eventually receives safe passage out of Hades and returns home, where he is ultimately reunited with his wife, as the hero King of Ithaca.

The second example is the movie, *The Matrix*. Our hero here is Thomas A. Anderson, played by Keanu Reeves. In the beginning, we meet Mr. Anderson as a boring cubicle-dwelling programmer who supplements his income by hacking into computers and selling stolen programs, under the alias Neo. During his excursions into the dark web, Neo's heard about this thing called the Matrix. He's curious about it but continues his drab and colorless ordinary life. Until one day, Trinity, played by Carrie Moss, gets him to meet with the mysterious Morpheus, played by Lawrence Fishburne. Morpheus ultimately presents Anderson/Neo with a choice: Take the blue pill and remain in his everyday boring life and forget about the Matrix or take the red pill and learn what the Matrix is.

Anderson/Neo chooses the red pill, and that's when the adventure begins. First, he discovers that the world he's been living in is a computer simulation concocted by machines that use incapacitated humans trapped in a virtual reality world, to produce the electric power they need to operate. The real world outside the Matrix is a post-nuclear apocalyptic wasteland. The few humans who remain free of the Matrix, live in an underground city, called Zion. There, they've banded together to fight the machines, pull people out of the simulation cage, and restore the real world. Anderson/Neo is believed to be a Messiah, who can bend the rules of the Matrix and defeat the machines. During the story, Anderson/Neo faces many challenges and doubts about this prophesy and his being this mythical savior. In the movie's final scenes, he is pursued by computer agents while he is on a mission in the Matrix and gunned down in an alley. All appears lost. Anderson/Neo is dead in the Matrix, and his physical body in the real world has flatlined. Everyone is distraught, but Trinity believes that he is the promised savior, called The One. She yells out to his dead body lying on a gurney in the real world, "Neo, get up!" Suddenly, his pulse returns in the real world, while in the Matrix, the dead figure opens his eyes and rises. He seems surprised at his resurrection and, upon looking at the world around him, plainly sees that it is not real. Upon seeing Anderson/Neo defy the laws of the Matrix and survive being shot, the agents all open fire on him. But he simply raises his hand in a stopping gesture and says, "No!" All the bullets stop in mid-air. Anderson/Neo plucks one up, curiously examines it, and then waves his hand, commanding all the shells to fall to the ground. Next, he easily defeats all the agents, who appeared unbeatable. At the end of the movie, he's seen back in the Matrix, where, after making a phone call to serve notice on the machine rulers of the Matrix, he effortlessly shows his new powers by flying straight up into the sky.

So, what common elements do you see in the ancient story of Odysseus and the modern-day hero Anderson/Neo more than two millennia later, that Campbell referred to in his research findings? Here they are:

1. Our future hero's story begins living an ordinary life in an everyday world.
2. The would-be hero receives a call to adventure.
3. At first, our future would-be hero is reluctant to leave the ordinary world they know.
4. Our hero meets a mentor or guide who encourages them to undertake the journey that leads to the hero's empowerment.
5. The future hero crosses the threshold and accepts the challenge.
6. The hero faces many tests, unknowns, forms allies, and enemies.
7. The hero approaches a final ordeal.
8. The hero faces the ordeal against what seems like impossible odds.
9. The triumphant hero receives their reward.
10. The hero now makes the journey back to the world where they formerly had their ordinary life.

11. Arriving back in the old world, the hero is a new, more powerful being with gifts for others.
12. The journey is completed.

Upon completing the twelve steps of this journey, many heroes become the mentor or guide that encourages and supports the next generation of heroes. Similar to how the hero, Luke Skywalker, played by Mark Hamill, ultimately became the mentor of Rey, in *The Last Jedi*. That is my goal in this book. As someone who benefited over many years from mentors during my hero's journey, I now wish to be your guide and mentor across your hero's journey.

Your Invitation to Adventure

Like our other past heroes, up until the end of 2019, you were living in an ordinary world of best practice sharing at conferences and a regular cadence of meetings and activities. Those came to an end in 2020. The pandemic, racial, social, and political unrest are your call to adventure. Like most emerging heroes of the past, your initial instinct is to hang on to the old world. We are now at step three. Here is where I invite you to leave the old ways behind and step forward into the journey ahead that I believe will take you and your efforts to a whole new level of success in creating more diverse, equitable, and inclusive organizations than ever before.

Of course, like all past heroes, you will need to face new challenges. These include:

- □ Entering a world where a new distributed workplace replaces the old model where 94 percent of your team members worked in the same company-owned building.
- □ A world with a new workforce where employees make up less than half the people on your team.
- □ A world where even essential workers can work from home, and their homes can be anywhere on the planet.
- □ A world where massive change happens all the time and comes at you faster every day. We are in the middle of a rapid expansion and confluence of technologies. Tools powered by AI, robotics,

and automation, quickly enter organizations and change how work gets done. Simultaneously, wearable technologies (like the Fitbit) and new ways of transferring currency (like cryptocurrency and the blockchain) change how people think about money, society, and even their physical well-being.

- A world where your company's fortunes and efforts can rise or fall at incredible speeds. In the first quarter of 2020, Ford Motors tallied up to two billion dollars in losses. Ford was not the only company that lost money that year, nor was it the most significant loss recorded. Fiat Chrysler burned through 5.5 billion. These types of losses weren't contained to the auto, airline, or any group of industries. It was across the board. Why? As Ford CEO, Jim Hackett put it, none of the companies had a disaster recovery plan titled Pandemic Business Plan. In short, they weren't ready to pivot.
- A world where vital decisions about your workforce, workplace, and marketplace that impact equity and inclusion are made by mysterious machines using hidden formulas that live outside the reach of unconscious bias or race relationship training workshops. Machines that can decide to hire and fire people without human intervention.

This book you're reading is the product of four years of research into the evolution of DEI (Diversity, Equity, and Inclusion) coupled with decades of an intense and passionate study of the philosophy and practices of playing to win in an arena full of unknowns. Its purpose is simple. To invite you to set forth on your hero's journey and equip you to succeed in this new world.

To that end, the seven chapters that make up this small one-hundred-and-fifty-page book are divided into three sections. The first section comprises chapters 2, 3, and 4. Chapter 2 will explore the history of our current DEI practices from their stormy birth in the 1960s up to 2019. There you will watch the evolution that layer by layer, built your practices, and shaped the demands placed on DEI and resource group leaders until the beginning of the COVID19 pandemic. Chapter 3 will look at why you need to turn your full attention to the future and stop waiting to go back to the past. Finally, we will end this section in chapter 4, where I will give you a peek into the future and teach you how to anticipate what's coming at you so you can prepare using the best practices employed by futurists.

Next, we will go to section two of the book. Section two is made up of two chapters. Chapter 5 contains ten tips that will enable resource group leaders to prepare their communities for the future. Likewise, chapter 6 includes ten tips for DEI leaders to prepare their entire practice for the future. I recommend you read both chapters, regardless of whether you lead the overall DEI function or a resource group. At a minimum, I urge you to read the one most applicable to you. As Kenneth Rogoff, Professor of Economics at Harvard, put it, "Having a business model which is flexible and adaptable was already very important in a world which is highly globalized and competitive with constant technological change. It is ten times as important right now." Like other parts of your organization, you need to make sure your DEI practices are fault-tolerant in the face of future pandemic-like disruptions and able to continue to pivot, evolve, and thrive."

The final section of this book has only one chapter. That chapter invites you to look at the future through a new lens where you seek to advance the cause of DEI, whether confronted by opportunity or challenge. Its goal is to make you unstoppable no matter what circumstances come your way.

As formal DEI leaders and leaders of resource groups, I believe that you've been living in the ordinary world before the end of 2019 and the beginning of 2020. You've also received a call to a new and wonderful adventure. This is your call to your hero's journey. Many of you, as heroes of the past, have been reluctant to leave the old world behind. In some cases, you may have been "trying to hold down the fort" until things returned to the old normal. But in truth, there is no going back to the way things were.

The stage for your journey is set. In 2020 a pandemic, social, political unrest called you to face an amazing adventure. The challenges you've been forced to face and those still to come are unprecedented. I now present you with a choice. It's a choice like the one Morpheus offered to Anderson/Neo. Take the blue pill and go back to focusing on the old best practices and waiting for things to go back to a fairytale "normal" of the past. Or accept the invitation to your hero's journey and take the red pill. And let's embark on the transformative journey that awaits us. I wholeheartedly invite you to take the red pill and turn the page.

PART I

Understanding the Past and Shaping the Future

DEI is a fascinating topic that has taken on a variety of meanings to represent different things over time. In the three chapters in this section of the book, we start by examining historical events that formed one of the critical pillars of the modern-day DEI practice: employee resource groups. We will look at how the evolution of these groups resulted in changes in the skills their leaders needed to bring to the table. Finally, we will look at where we are now, where we are going, and how modern-day DEI leaders need to shift their thinking to continue moving forward in this new world of rapid change and disruption.

CHAPTER 2

The Path That Brought Us to Our Current State

"In the midst of chaos, there is also opportunity."–***Sun-Tzu, The Art of War***

The story of today's DEI practices begins with the birth of the Employee Resource Group (ERG). Today's company ERGs are made up of employees who form or join groups in their workplace based on identification with others like themselves who share either common social characteristics or life experiences. ERGs are traditionally focused on underrepresented groups identified by: race, ethnicity, gender, age, sexual orientation, disability, veterans, etc. Most recently, some ERGs are expanding to "interest-based" groups. For example, we have multicultural and multigenerational group activities such as social justice advocacy, workplace wellness, family caregiving, etc. In most organizations, membership is voluntary and open to all employees.

Employee resource groups are called by various names in different organizations. Some companies refer to them as Affinity Groups, others call them business resource groups (BRGs). In some literature, the terms affinity group, employee resource group, and business resource group are used to talk about the progression of these associations over time. Among those three labels, there is a long list of other names used in firms worldwide. In this book, we will call them all ERG for uniformity and simplicity since it is the most widely used term to refer to these groups.

To understand the development and trajectory of ERGs and their leaders, we need to go back to the beginning. And that beginning takes us to the hot summer day of July 24, 1964, in Rochester, NY. The temperature was in the 80s. There was a block party with about two hundred people on Nassau Street, near Joseph Avenue. According to a man named William Turner, who was at the event, the city had sent one police cruiser just to cordon off the streets so that no cars could come through and to keep an eye on things. A young Black man named Randy Manigault, had a little too much to drink, as young people everywhere are apt to do in a party atmosphere. Randy's friends wanted to take him home. The police tried to take him to jail.

When the police tried to arrest him, Manigault resisted, and the officers became more forceful. Bystanders who felt the police were overly aggressive started throwing bottles, rocks, and bricks at the police. The police called for backup, and a K-9 unit responded. Two police dogs were used to control the crowd. This use of dogs seems to have played a part in igniting the crowd. The presence of the dogs evoked memories of violent police dogs used against peaceful civil rights protesters in Birmingham, Alabama. By 11:30 pm, all available officers were deployed and engaged with around 400 rioters. At 2:00 am, the Rochester police chief ordered officers to use riot weapons on the crowd. The riot swelled to 2,000 people by 3:30 am. At 9:00 am July 25, New York's Governor declared a state of emergency, and the event was officially categorized as a "riot." By the time, the riot was over, five people were dead, over 350 people were injured, and almost a thousand people were arrested [(1)].

White residents of Rochester were surprised by this riot because of the city's history of progressive 19th-century politics. A large part of Rochester's history revolved around the Underground Railroad and its well-known resident abolitionist, Fredrick Douglass, and women's rights activist, Susan B. Anthony. Both were buried in the city's Mount Hope cemetery. But these perceptions on the part of the White community of Rochester ignored a growing tension beneath the surface.

These tensions were fueled by a demographic shift in the population of Rochester. The Black population of Rochester had grown during the 1950s and 1960s from 7,845 to more than 32,000 people. That's almost four times growth. Most of that migration came from people traveling from the South to the North in hopes of better conditions. But instead, Black migrants were met with segregated schools, dilapidated buildings, and a tremendous unemployment rate. (Six times higher than the unemployment rate for whites). Black residents also suffered from constant public harassment and humiliation. They were referred to as "bean pickers," denied housing throughout the city, and funneled into the run-down Upper Falls neighborhood [(2)].

Large companies in the area, like Xerox and Kodak, saw all this tension as threatening to the reputations of their burgeoning corporate hubs in Rochester. Leaders in these companies felt investments in Black-owned businesses and jobs for the growing Black population might be an antidote to racial unrest.

Amid all this tension, Joseph C. Wilson, a local businessman and the Chairman of Xerox, took the steps that led to the formation of what has evolved into the modern-day ERG. Joseph Chamberlain Wilson was born in Rochester. At the time of these events, he was 55 years old. Watching Wilson with his Clark Kent glasses and suit, and slick back short dark hair, speaking at an employee orientation in a video, I got the impression that he was an inspirational leader. He talked about his company paying a premium on imagination and creativity, not people who wanted to do things tomorrow the same way they had done them yesterday [(3)].

Xerox was founded in 1906 in Rochester, New York, as The Haloid Photographic Company. It manufactured photographic paper and equipment used to make copies. Wilson took over Haloid from his father and, in 1946, signed an agreement to develop it as a commercial product [(4)]. The bulk of the company's operations and employees were in Rochester, NY, during the riots.

In attempts to address the underlying issues driving unrest in Rochester, Wilson wrote letters to his managers calling for them to increase the hiring of African Americans. One of those hires included Ursula Burns, who later became the first Black woman to lead a Fortune 500 company as its chief executive officer. He also met with community activists to explore the opportunity for black-owned and -operated manufacturing companies. These could provide both new pride and new jobs. To help ensure their confidence in success, Wilson assured them Xerox would be a customer for these new Black-owned businesses. As part of this effort, Xerox teamed up with a Black power group to create a factory that made vacuums and other parts for copying and film processing that was partly owned by its workforce. That company was later named Eltrex Industries. It provided hundreds of manufacturing jobs to the Black community members in Rochester [(5)].

Wilson and Xerox began to tap into emerging Black caucus groups to generate all these new progressive ideas within the company. These were joined by other caucus groups, which became the precursor to the modern-day ERG. That was the first spark that ignited the development of the modern ERG.

Other ERGs quickly formed across the organization. These were the beginnings of the broad array of cultural and special interest groups we see today. They included Latinos, women, and other demographics. The primary mission of these early groups was to provide comfort, camaraderie, a platform to share the common experiences of workplace exclusion and marginalization of their members, and pool together resources toward activist solutions. The leaders of these groups needed to have good community organizing skills. Skills like empathy, building membership, running meetings, and eliciting, collecting, and summarizing group ideas, to name a few. It also took a certain amount of courage to lead these groups back then, in the face of subtle and not-so-subtle opposition.

The Second Spark That Shaped the Modern ERG

Over the next few years, more ERGs appeared across the business landscape. The expansion of ERGs as a practice resulted in the development of several associations designed to recognize and reward the leaders of these groups. Many of these include well-known ones like the National Affinity Leadership Congress and The Association of ERGs. Leaders of these groups enjoyed the recognition and support from these outside organizations and the positive feedback they got from their members.

One of my good friends, author Simone Morris, talks about how being an ERG leader was a "life raft" for her when she was in a career slump. Morris is a tall African American female who, today, runs a consulting practice. In speaking about her past role in ERGs, she refers to it as a "game-changing experience" in her career. An experience where, in her words, she discovered "the power of using her voice [6]."

But while many group leaders and members felt good about being part of their employee associations, the greater corporate community over the years started to view them as a "nice" company-sanctioned social club. One person I ran into years ago called them "extracurricular activity to keep the disenfranchised happy and quiet." Some people who could potentially join an ERG questioned the value they would get out of investing their time. "How is membership going to help me get visibility or a promotion," was a common question." These perspectives were often thought to be behind the underfunding and lack of more significant groundswell of support for these groups.

In response to this, in the early 1990s, many groups expanded their mission. They began to include more serious levels of professional development and career counseling. Often, they would partner with their companies' Talent Develop Department to design and roll out mentoring and sponsorship programs. They also introduced the practice of corporate cultural celebration month events designed to raise workplace awareness and appreciation of the contributions of their respective cultures to the United States, their industries, and organizations. This shift, of course, increased the skills and resources needed to be an effective ERG leader. It was no longer enough to be a good community organizer. On top of that, leaders needed to be good at partnering across the organization, influencing members of a leadership group to stage events, finding and booking developmental speakers, etc. Around the same time, to rebrand themselves, many groups dropped the word affinity from their names and started calling themselves employee resource groups.

Despite the rebranding and the additional layers of value, many groups found that they were still primarily viewed as a nice-to-have extracurricular activity for underrepresented employees. So shortly after that, in the mid to late 1990s, several groups began adding another layer of value. These were spurred on by stories of ERGs that had scored big business wins for their companies and were getting attention from their

CEOs and other senior leaders. Many decided to rebrand themselves again, calling themselves Business Resource Groups. These third-stage ERGs focused on driving their companies' financial, reputational, and other forms of value. Some of these groups, such as the Novartis Culture Clubs, generated over a billion US dollars for their company. These group leaders now needed to add another layer of skills on top of what the earlier groups demanded. These ERG leaders needed a keen understanding of their core business and the insight to know where and how to direct the group to drive measurable business value.

So, in summary, there were two critical moments and factors that gave us the modern ERG. The first was an activist response to the racial tensions of the 1960s. The other was the increasing efforts by ERG group leaders to drive more value and acquire more recognition and support from their organizations. And that has been the path for several decades, until now.

The Ignitors of the Third Spark That's Driving the Reshaping of ERGs into the Future

On January 4, 2020, my wife and I flew on a packed American Airlines flight to the island of St Kitts. This was part of an annual migration pattern for us. We had discovered the island during a cruise many years before and vowed to return for a more extended stay. That one-month stay introduced us to several new and dear friends from around the world and made our two-month annual visits a regular part of our lives. That year, our trip to St Kitts was like any other. Full of beaches, fun, and days in the comfortable low 80s weather and far from our home's cold, snowy streets in New York City. Toward the end of our trip, stories began to reach us about a mysterious illness in China. Occasionally our gaggle of friends would speculate on what might be the cause. One of our friends had been to Wuhan, China, and agreed with the idea that perhaps this new disease had jumped from the bats in the "wet markets" to humans in the community. The conversation smoothly moved on to an upcoming beach party.

On the morning of February 26, my wife and I met with our friends for a final coffee in the outdoor shop, covered by the bright red and yellow awning across from a golf course. We drank coffee, hugged our friends, and talked about seeing some of them in Europe later on a planned trip that year. Our first clue that something had dramatically changed came when we boarded our flight home that afternoon. The plane was half empty. We were sitting in a three-seat row. As I always do, I gave my wife the window seat (She loves the window). I sat in the middle. Next to me was a man in his late 40s of medium build with short brown thinning hair. He was visibly shaken by having to sit next to a stranger on this four-hour trip home. It wasn't until I got back home and started following the news more carefully that I became more keenly aware of the deadliness of this new disease. I also realized that no one was safe from it. It was a global pandemic, not a local problem in China and parts of Europe. In the weeks and months that followed, I saw my gym close, companies sending 35 percent of their workforce into remote work, and our trips to the supermarket replaced by Instacart deliveries.

Hunkered down in our home, we didn't think things could get worse. Then on May 25, 2020, an African American man was murdered by a police officer in Minneapolis, Minnesota. It all started when a store clerk suspected George Floyd may have used a counterfeit $20 bill. The clerk called the police. One of four police officers who arrived on the scene, Derek Chauvin, knelt on Floyd's neck and back for 9 minutes and 29 seconds. Floyd's brutal and callous murder was filmed on a video that was played repeatedly on the Internet and television. It sparked a wave of protests against police brutality towards Black people that quickly spread across the United States and globally. Floyd's dying words, "I can't breathe," became their rallying cry.

While Floyd's murder sparked these street protests, several other underlying incidents served as kindling wood. Some of the better-known ones involved Ahmaud Arbery and Breonna Taylor. Arbery was a 25-year-old Black man out jogging when two armed White men chased and shot him in a South Georgia neighborhood on February 23, 2020. Less than a month later, Breonna Taylor, a Black medical worker, was shot and killed in her home by Louisville, Kentucky police in a botched March 13, 2020, raid. Corporations that had been cutting back on their diversity, equity, and inclusion budgets and letting DEI staff go as part of battening down the financial hatches, suddenly had to shift gears and start investing more heavily in DEI. They found themselves in the gaping hole of the perfect storm coming at them from all sides. A double whammy of disruption as the health pandemic and the underlying racial crisis crashed into each other. They were not ready for a jump from 6 percent to 35 percent remote work, traumatized employees, working mothers without childcare or schools, and a whole host of other disruptive situations. It was into that breach that corporate ERGs jumped in to save the day and begin their journey towards their third transformation.

What Have ERGs and Their Leaders Been Doing Since the Beginning of Early 2020?

October 21, 2021, my DEI leadership development association held our annual CDO PowerCircle Future Foresight Summit. The two-day summit was originally planned for an in-person meeting. But like many other best-laid plans, we had to rethink our strategy as we watched rising COVID19 cases. So, we pivoted over to Zoom.

The CDO PowerCircle is an association of top Chief Diversity Officers from companies worldwide. These companies collectively generate nearly three-quarters of a trillion US dollars with almost one million employees. Member organizations are from various industries, including finance, healthcare, insurance, manufacturing, and entertainment. Their representatives are seasoned DEI leaders. This summit aims to explore how the world and DEI practices are changing and to set strategies for the emerging future. One of the summit's panels this year focused on ERGs and how they were responding to challenges in this new world order. Here are the highlights of what the panel revealed.

The discussion was led by my friend, Andres Gonzalez, a Latinx leader, who is the CDO of Froedtert Health, located in Wisconsin. Gonzalez is slightly over six feet in height with a trim goatee and mustache and friendly eyes that are the embodiment of servant leadership. Despite all his accomplishments, his mannerisms balance confidence combined with personal humility, respect, and kindness towards others. His panelists are Dionna Gavin, Director of Diversity and Inclusion at Froedtert; Kate

Longfield, Director of Diversity at Dollar General; and Fran Parr, a Group Modeling Delivery Manager at Hiscox and the co-Lead of a Hiscox ERG.

Gonzalez opened by framing the discussion to explore what ERGs were doing in light of the pandemic, economic stress, and social unrest. His first question went to his Froedtert colleague, Dionna Gavin. He asked her to share how she saw the ERGs at Froedtert responding.

Gavin is an African American woman with a Master of Education degree who also completed an African American Leadership Program. I've never had the pleasure of meeting her in person, but my impression of her based-on Zoom meetings is that she is also a confident and humble leader like Gonzalez. "Being a healthcare facility, we were hit very hard," she said by way of an opening response. She then shared how the ERGs, together with the diversity council, had focused their efforts on addressing the human side of the pandemic in the community and trying to get people to come in for vaccines.

One of the biggest obstacles that prevent people from getting vaccinated in many communities is their long history of mistreatment. For example, take the experience of the Black community, from gruesome experiments on enslaved people to the forced sterilizations of Black women and the infamous Tuskegee syphilis study that withheld treatment from hundreds of Black men for decades to let doctors track the course of the disease. So, it's not surprising that there is a lot of distrust in those communities of people who are in healthcare. Michael Che, one of the stars of *Saturday Night Live*, gave voice to the thinking of many in the Black community when he said, "I've got mixed feelings about the vaccine. On the one hand, I'm Black, so naturally, I don't trust it. But on the other hand, I'm on a white TV show so that I might get the real one."

Or let's look at the Latinx community. Many Latinx people are also distrustful of healthcare professionals. Some, undocumented, are afraid the doctor or hospital will expose them and result in deportation away from family members. Others prefer to use homemade remedies. Whatever the reason, the facts are clear: Latinos are one of the racial and ethnic groups that are among the least likely to trust and visit doctors.

For healthcare organizations like Froedtert, trying to protect a diverse community from a deadly disease, this presents a considerable challenge.

This is the human side that Gavin was talking about. This is where she found Froedtert's diversity council, chaired by their CEO, Catherine Jacobson, and their ERGs took decisive action. That powerful action took form in a series of internal panel discussions involving the Chief Medical Officer and the ERGs around community fears and hesitancy. These engaged ERGs acted as trusted intermediaries to communicate to staff in all roles and across all dimensions of diversity, how to stay safe and healthy, inclusively and equitably. They also helped identify stories and produce public engagement with the community to understand the pandemic's impact and the needs of the diverse populations Froedtert serves. These communications and reports designed to eliminate vaccine hesitancy found their way into public service announcements and other tools to gain community trust. Gavin's modesty prevented her from mentioning that these efforts earned Froedtert a Top Ten Diversity Action Award, in 2021.

As I listened to Gavin speak, I became keenly aware of the full impact of her story. These ERGs were acting as a community liaison for the hospital. As Gonzalez summed up, they were acting as ambassadors for their organization and a two-way line of communication during a crisis. The impact of what they were doing was measured in something more valuable than money and bottom-line results. It was saving countless human lives that would have otherwise been lost. I was still a bit awe-struck by this revelation of ERGs as lifesavers when Gonzalez called on Kate Longfield.

Longfield is another colleague whom I haven't had the pleasure of meeting in person. Longfield holds a Master of Leadership Development and Organizational Development degree. She is a White female who projects an easy-going friendliness and openness to learning from others. As you listen to her speak, you realize that her experience and perception go a lot deeper than you would immediately guess by her light demeanor. In her opening response to Gonzalez, she notes that it's her role to ensure that her company supports the needs of all its employees and that she is keenly aware that she needs the ERGs to do that. Why? Because just like Froedtert's CEO, once told me, Longfield realizes that the ERG leaders and members "know stuff we don't know." Longfield then proceeded to share two strong examples of what the Dollar Generals ERGs have done for the organization and its employees during this time of disruption. For example, the African American community led the design and release of an allyship guide to help address the concerns of civil and social unrest. Another group representing the Young Professional Community focused on creating a cultural and social support environment for remote Dollar General employees. Again, these are activities that fill organizational gaps. Both cases create new resources needed by the organization to fill an emerging need.

Longfield also identified a silver lining in the pandemic cloud that forced many employees into remote work. Like most organizations, she explained, in the past, Dollar Generals ERGs focused on events and efforts that served their in-the-office community primarily. Once they lost the ability to bring everyone together in one place, as Longfield put it, "we had to think out of the box." That out-of-the-box thinking led the ERGs to realize that they could expand their tent since meetings are now online. Instead of inviting only the people in the home office, they could now ask all the 157,000 people who work for Dollar General across all locations to join them. They could also record these events and make them available for watch parties composed of people working on different shifts. These efforts extended speaker events, mentoring circles, and other opportunities to the entire organization. This, in effect, created what Froedtert CEO, Catherine Jacobson and I spoke about earlier in the year on an ERG PowerTalk podcast interview. It turned the ERGs into cultural life rafts for the distributed organization.

Finally, Gonzalez called on Fran Parr. Parr is a White female living in the UK whose day job is not in the DEI space. She describes herself as a pragmatic, highly driven, and enthusiastic IT delivery manager with ten years of experience in the insurance industry, in her LinkedIn profile. Not surprisingly, her education is in the not-so-fuzzy field of mathematics. Parr, however, is also the co-Leader of a group dedicated to the mental health and well-being of Hiscox employees, called WeMind. Parr is the third-panel member that I have not met in person. Like the others, however, I find her to be friendly and eminently modest about what I consider vital and precious.

Parr opened her comments by sharing a brief overview of her group's work. This includes providing monthly mental health tips for her organization's employees and raising awareness of different events, like breast cancer awareness. Parr and her group were in the middle of testing remote work when the pandemic began. During the trial, they got the notice saying, "Okay. From now you are all working from home for the foreseeable future." This was something where Hiscox had little experience. "We had a crisis meeting with the WeMind Committee," states Parr. They decided to do the following out of this meeting: One, go from monthly mental health communications to weekly publications. And two, focus more heavily on addressing the concerns around the daily news on the pandemic. These were used to help employees cope with health anxieties, the disruptions of working from home with partners and children who were also going to school remotely, and not seeing family and friends. In addition to this, her community committee shared personal stories that connected with the readers. And on top of all that, the committee ran online speaking events with engaging speakers on several mental and emotional health topics. Parr's group also provided just-in-time communication using tools like "WhatsApp and Yammer." The goal was simple. Make sure that people in this crisis did not feel alone and unsupported.

Gonzalez, picking up the emerging theme that tells us that ERGs seem to be at the forefront of taking care of more than the professional person, asked the panel to delve a bit deeper into the new aspect of ERG work. Longfield acknowledged how much Dollar General is currently relying on its ERGs to identify specific personal needs because, as she puts it, "they know what's going on with their community." She went on to explain how she and members of HR are asking the ERGs, "What does your community need, and how do we make that happen for you?"

Longfield went on to supply some examples. One of these conversations with the women's ERG led to a joint effort with the benefits team on how female professionals could effectively cope with the extra burdens they faced working from home, often with husbands and school-age children. They also had a session on dealing with breast cancer while working from home, as well as coping with the stress of being the caregiver of a loved one with cancer. Another area where Longfield tells us Dollar General has leveraged their ERGs is to bring together the various sub-communities represented by the ERGs. The goal here is to support what she calls "the whole person." As noted by Longfield, people generally fall into more than one diversity bucket. For example, someone could be a Black-female-veteran. So, holding joint events resulting from collaboration between several ERGs was used by Dollar General to address these intersectional needs.

Gavin added that Froedtert has also focused on this new model of supporting the whole person. One example she shares involved having meetings with ERG communities to let them talk about what is happening instead of inviting them to attend a meeting just to listen to speakers on a topic. "Instead of having meetings around a specific topic, it was more of a let's check in with the members," according to Gavin. One instance of this, Gavin tells us, took place during Black History Month. The theme of the meeting was The Black Communities Mental Health During These Turbulent Times. Instead of having a licensed psychologist speak, they turned the event into a community conversation. This new approach enables Froedtert to determine how the events outside of work influence team members and what specific resources and support these community members need.

At this point in the discussion, as we neared the end, Gonzalez shifted the panel's attention to how ERGs are currently supporting the continuing development of their communities, professionally, in this new environment. Longfield took the lead on that question. She spoke about how Dollar General realized the growing role of ERGs in the professional development of their members and in aligning their members to the business. Longfield noted that to do this, companies like hers had to invest more in the development and training of their ERG leaders. One way that she highlighted Dollar General was doing this, was by leveraging the ERG leadership development tools of the CDO PowerCircle and the ERG PowerTalk podcast.

Parr added that ERG communities support talent development by enabling members to explore and grow skills through their ERG work. "We encourage everyone on our committee to have something in their objectives about their work on the committee," states Parr. Despite this being something done beyond the scope of the work they were hired to do; it is upskilling and developmental.

Gavin rounded out this discussion segment by sharing how Froedtert leverages running these groups to develop the skills of group leaders intentionally. "What do you want to get out of it," Gavin tells us is a common question they ask leaders and members of groups at Froedtert. She tells us this to ensure that the experience is tied to the individual's personal business development goals. Gavin also talked about how Froedtert connects ERG work to the leader's performance development plan.

Another fascinating detail that Gavin shares is the executive sponsor's expanding role in these new ERGs. Instead of just being "The Executive Representative for the ERG," the sponsors of these ERGs are deeply involved in the development of the community. At Froedtert, Gavin tells us, ERG Executive Sponsors are liaisons to external boards of the communities supported by the ERG, developmental coaches to the leaders, mentors, and talent scouts.

As the conversation begins to wind down, Gonzalez focuses them on the new rewards coming to the ERG leader. Longfield again takes point here and talks about how the leaders of her ERGs have the ear of the CEO. This increase in appreciation and visibility of the value provided by ERGs has led to discussions around how to better support them and even compensate their leadership.

Longfield is touching here on two themes that I've been hearing repeatedly since mid-2020. More CEOs are now connecting directly with the ERG leaders in their organizations. As Wilson did, close to six decades ago, these CEOs see the value of collecting and responding to these diverse perspectives. And as for exploring compensating ERG leaders, that, too, is increasing. According to one of my podcast guests, Jes Osrow, co-Founder and COO of the Rise Journey, the number of companies compensating

ERG leaders went up from six percent to twenty-eight percent in the past year [7].

So here is a summary of what we learned about what ERGs have done in response to the significant shifts that started in early 2020:

1. ERGs have embraced their role as their companies' ambassadors to the internal and external diverse communities they represent. As such, they provide an essential glue needed to tie together all the perspectives of various stakeholders and enable business leaders to make better decisions.
2. ERGs have extended and protected the company culture from collapse as people had to bail out and abandon the corporate offices. By linking their members across silo lines, they provide communities of connections that replace the old pre-pandemic physical work campuses.
3. ERGs have gone beyond supporting the professional individual to supporting the whole person. This is important, because as Parr put it, "we humans cannot shut the door on our stresses and make-believe, they're not there" when we go to work. She also shared a global statistic that tells us that we've gone from one in four people having mental health issues to one in two. [illegible] hit the nail on the head when he stated that supporting the whole person more effectively, may very well be one of the biggest success differentiators for companies that want to attract, engage, and leverage the best people in the new normal.
4. ERGs are increasingly becoming even more critical professional development components for group members and leaders.
5. The role of the ERG Executive Sponsor is also evolving to meet and support the needs of the new ERG leader and community. The new executive sponsors are more than just the group's executive representative.
6. No big surprise, given the more prominent role ERGs are playing in this new normal, an increasing number of ERG leaders are getting more attention from their CEOs.

7. Along with this senior-level attention, a growing number of companies are compensating their ERG leaders for their extraordinary and vital efforts.

For years there was a great deal of talk about the need for flexible and adaptive organizations. Unfortunately, most of this was just talk. While academics and speakers droned on about agile organizations at HR and business conferences, most attendee organizations continued to operate the way they had for the last few decades. Some tried to apply their traditional leadership committee approaches to these challenges, but as one CEO put it to me, “they were flying blind.” Blind due to the lack of diversity of voices at the table and their collective blind spots. Meanwhile, these little groups, called ERGs that had started in the 1960s, slowly evolved inside these organizations. From their early roots as activists through their maturity into employee and business support resources, they mainly sat underutilized in many but a few companies. Until 2020 rolled in and turned the world upside down.

Just like it took a monumental event to bring ERGs into existence, it took another massive event to get them to center stage. But this is only the beginning. In chapter four, we will look at the disruptive events lurking just around the corner that promise to hurl you and your ERGs deeper into the 21st-century vortex of challenges and opportunities. Hold on to your hats. The biggest waves of turbulence are yet to come!

But before we go there, in the next chapter, let’s take a moment to focus on why you should care about the future. Why is it so vital? What do you need to do to prepare yourself to avoid obstacles and get the most out of opportunities?

Chapter Bibliography

1. 1964 Rochester Riots. https://en.wikipedia.org/wiki/1964_Rochester_race_riot.
2. The First Black Settlers Who Shaped Rochester's Minority Neighborhoods. s.l. : Southwest Tribune, September 3, 2019. https://southwesttribune.com/news/first-black-settlers-shaped-rochesters-minority-neighborhoods/.
3. Joe Wilson Inspirational Speech: Xerox Employee Orientation. s.l. : Xerox, November 14, 2006. https://www.youtube.com/watch?v=Hc6_BWXXCos.
4. Xerox. s.l. : Wikipedia. https://en.wikipedia.org/wiki/Xerox#:~:text=Xerox%20was%20founded%20in%201906,manufactured%20photographic%20paper%20and%20equipment.&text=Haloid%20changed%20its%20name%20to,then%20Xerox%20Corporation%20in%201961.
5. Diversity at Xerox. s.l. : Xerox. https://www.xerox.com/downloads/usa/en/n/nr_Xerox_Diversity_Timeline_2008.pdf.
6. How ERG Membership Ignites Your Passion. s.l. : ERG PowerTalk Podcast, April 20, 2020.
7. How to be Adequately Compensated as an ERG Leader. s.l. : ERG PowerTalk. Interview for the episode to be released in 2022.

CHAPTER 3

Why Should You Care About the Future?

"My interest is in the future because I am going to spend the rest of my life there."– ***Charles Kettering***

In 1975, a 24-year-old American engineer, born in Brooklyn New York, invented a product that would revolutionize his industry. His name is Steven J. Sasson. Sasson was a graduate of Rensselaer Polytechnic Institute. Back then, Sasson sported slightly long blond hair that covered most of his ears and framed a young intelligent face [(1)].

Shortly after he graduated from college, Sasson took a job at Kodak, in 1973. He worked in a small research lab in Kodak's apparatus division under a supervisor named Gareth Lloyd. According to Sasson, his journey toward his game-changing invention started in 1974 when Lloyd gave him a choice between working on one of two small projects. One was to look at the exposure controls for movie cameras. The other was to look at the performance of new devices called charge-coupled device imagers. This second project involved exploring the possibility of building a camera that used only solid-state imagers and created a completely digital picture. "In college, I'd done some work on optically controlled silicon devices, and so I was interested in how light affected silicon. I jumped at the chance to work with this new device," said Sasson in a 2008 interview [(2)]. So Sasson was off to the races.

By Autumn of 1975, Sasson was ready to unveil his findings to a group of research colleagues at Eastman Kodak's headquarters, in Rochester, New York. The title of Sasson's presentation was "Film-less Photography." In the presentation, he demonstrated a working model for the first digital camera. The device was the size of a toaster and captured black-and-white photos on a digital cassette tape. The image took about 23 seconds to record onto the cassette and another 23 seconds to read off a playback unit onto a television. Then, something amazing happened: a grainy black-and-white image appeared on the TV screen. Digital photography was born.

Kodak executives watched the process and they yawned. They were convinced that no one would ever want to look at their pictures on a screen. They felt print's been with us for over a hundred years. No one is complaining about it. It's a best practice. So why they wondered, would anybody want to look at pictures on a TV screen?

At the time of Sasson's presentation, Kodak had 85% of the market share in cameras and 90% of the market share in film. They were the industry's eight-hundred-pound gorilla. Thirty-seven years later, on January 19th, 2012, Kodak filed for Chapter Eleven bankruptcy. Why? Because they failed to leverage their advantage as the inventors of digital photography and their competitors beat them to the punch.

Kodak, of course, is not dead. Sasson, now 71 years old is still there. But the company has never risen back to its former size and power. These days, it's used as a cautionary tale for business students.

But what exactly was the failure? Surely, we are not saying that Kodak's leadership should have been able to foresee the future. Of course not. No one can do that. But what any leader worth their salt needs to be able to do to stay competitive is have the vision and foresight to effectively navigate themselves and their team through the near- and long-term future. You might say that good leaders of groups of any size are futurists.

Why you need to be a futurist

Being a leader who is a futurist is especially important today. As noted by Futurist and podcaster, Jacob Morgan in his book, *The Future Leader: 9 Skills and Mindsets to Succeed in the Next Decade.* According to Morgan, being a futurist is one of the five essential skills leaders need more than ever today [(3)]. Why? Because the speed of disruption is speeding up.

You don't need me to give you a long lecture on how the speed of change has been speeding up. If you work in any capacity for a company,

I'm sure the mind-numbing meetings and constant buzz of activity have made that point. And every indicator is that things will continue to move even faster and become more complex. New technologies, automation, global competition, and more will make sure of that. (More on how some of these factors will impact your world and your ERGs in another chapter). You no longer have the luxury of a decade ago, to "watch what's happening and then figure out what to do." The best analogy for what is required of you as an ERG or DEI leader, or any leader for that matter, is like what faces a major league baseball hitter at bat, with a fastball coming their way.

At hundred miles an hour, that ball will close the gap between the pitcher's mound and the batter at home plate in approximately three hundred and seventy-five milliseconds. If you want to get a picture of how long we are talking about, that's the speed at which we blink. The hitter's reaction time, where his brain tells his arms to swing, is two hundred fifty milliseconds. That leaves the player at bat with only an impossible one hundred and twenty-five milliseconds for his brain to communicate the ball's approach and decide if the ball is within the strike zone. It takes almost one hundred of those precious milliseconds for the brain to just communicate the ball moving in their direction to the decision-making centers. To swing or not to swing is the twenty-five-millisecond question. If the batter waits until the ball's trajectory is completely clear, they will swing too late. But if they just pray and swing, it might just be a strike. There simply isn't enough time to assess the situation, communicate the facts, and make the decision to take the right action once the ball leaves the pitcher's hand [(4)].

This was the kind of situation that many ERG and DEI leaders found themselves in, at the beginning of the pandemic. As instructions to stay at home came along, many canceled their conferences and meetings. Meanwhile, others, like Froedtert, soldiered on. In an episode of ERG PowerTalk that aired March 23, 2020, at the beginning of the lockdown, I spoke with the person, who at the time was a Director of Diversity and Inclusion at Froedtert. She explained how right around the time the pandemic was heating up, her company was planning the launch of a new ERG for women in leadership at Froedtert. They wanted to have the event in March, which happens to be Women's History Month. They had a little over 60 people registered for the event. On the very day of the event, the recommendations were issued in the state of Wisconsin limiting the size of gatherings. "We had to pivot very quickly," she stated. What an understatement. But pivot they did. They turned the entire event into a virtual live stream panel discussion. They even found a way to run a planned raffle successfully over digital technology. All in less than twenty-four hours. That has to be right up there with hitting a ball coming at you at a hundred miles an hour. Furthermore, she told us they recorded the event and made it available to an even broader audience of shift workers. So, a bonus to boot.

But how did they do it? Before we answer that, let's go back to the ballgame. How do major league batters hit those fastballs? Well, it turns out they have two secret weapons at their disposal. When you watch a hitter like twenty-eight-year-old Trea Turner of the Los Angeles Dodgers hit that ball 32.8 percent of the time, you are seeing two invisible forces at play. First major league hitters like turner have above-average eyesight. According to studies, major league hitters have incredible visual acuity. Eighty-one percent of these players have 20/15 vision, 2% have 20/9.2 and the overall average is 20/13. Similar results were noted on distance stereo acuity testing of their eyes. Stereo acuity refers to the range of differences between how one eye and the other see an object in the distance. The smaller the difference, the greater the acuity score. The bottom line is that these players have eyesight that sharply exceeds that of the average population (5). This superior vision lets the hitter clearly see the way the pitcher is prepping and setting up to throw the ball from the mound sixty feet and six inches away. So, there is a structural component here that enables the various parts of this player's body and brain to communicate better in a fast-moving environment.

The second secret weapon is experience and training. By the time you see a major league player on home plate, they've been playing for several years. Some from high school and others even earlier. After that, through college and minor leagues. They have at least the ten thousand hours of practice, if not more, that Malcolm Gladwell talks about in his book, *Blink*. Over time, players, like Turner, have developed their ability to predict the type of pitch and the trajectory that's coming at them, through the moves that the pitcher makes when they're basically setting up to throw the ball. The rest is pure stadium magic.

Returning now to our ERG and DEI leaders, we can see how these two elements of a superior communication structure and the ability to read the tea leaves come into play. If you tune into the entire interview with Froedtert's Director of Diversity, and other interviews I've done on the podcast with Froedtert CDO, Andres Gonzalez, you will know that they are a highly connected group. By highly connected, I mean that their structure is linked and aligned in a manner that enables information to travel from group leaders through various levels of management and back, very quickly. For example, their ERG executive sponsors sit on external boards that support communities, like the ones represented by the group they advocate for in the company, as well as sitting on the CEOs' business table and diversity council. The communication distance between ERGs and the CEO is one very short hop away. So, information moves very quickly through the company. That is like having a brain that has the benefit of 20/13 vision.

Second, Froedtert's ERGs and DEI practices are tech-savvy. Froedtert has been using tech tools like Workbook, a product from Facebook (now known as Meta) to connect all their ERG groups together for years. So, while the need to urgently do this was indeed a pressing matter, they had the experience under their belt to muster a quick response. Like our major league baseball players, they were able to communicate all the facts quickly and had the experience to come up with a just-in-time solution. These elements are at the center of how ERGs, their leaders, and organizations can develop their futurist abilities.

Before we talk about that though, let's take a moment to explain more specifically what a futurist is and how they do their work. After that, I will show exactly how to develop your futurist abilities so that you can effortlessly swing for the fences, no matter what the future pitches at you.

What Do Futurists Do?

Roy Charles Amara was born on April 7, 1925. He was an American researcher, scientist, futurist, and president of the Institute for the Future. In addition to an impressive job, Amara had an equally impressive background. He held a BS in Management, an MS in the Arts and Sciences, and a Ph.D. in Systems Engineering. He also worked at the Stanford Research Institute. Pictures of Amara show a friendly smiling man with short white hair and an air of complete confidence. If ever there was a profile of a twentieth-century wizard, it might look exactly like Amara. In 1982, our confidant, highly credentialed, and wise futurist said the following in an article billed by the New York Times as a promised glimpse into the year 2000: "We'll be living in similar houses, except they'll be unquestionably smaller and more clustered. Birth rates will fall, and inflation will get worse. Workers will want intellectual and psychological fulfillment, not just financial reward."

In that same article, Herman Kahn, founder of the Hudson Institute, added his future thoughts. Kahn was born on February 15, 1922. He held a BA from the University of California, Los Angeles, and an MS from the California Institute of Technology. He was a preeminent futurist. Somewhat heavy set with a round face, thinning hair, and glasses, he offered another picture of the future world. According to Kahn, Inflation would soon be zero, He also predicted that per capita income would double. There would be no energy problems. Robots would be handling all the menial chores. And, for good measure, he added, expect lots of "family experimentation," including group marriages (8).

The Times article goes on to talk about how many of these predictions were wrong. But this article misses the whole point of what futurists do. First, futurists do not predict the future. Say what? So, what do they do, you may ask? The Association of Professional Futurists describes a "futurist" as one who studies the future to help people understand, anticipate, prepare for, and gain advantage from coming changes. Futurists do not predict what will happen; rather they describe what could happen."

Being a futurist leader involves doing three things. The first is to find and observe signals of new trends in your area of interest. There are futurist and futurist leaders across many disciplines. A quick look at a list of futurists in Wikipedia will include geopolitical authors, like Abishur Prakash through Buckminster Fuller the architect, cosmologist, whole-systems thinker, and inventor to Ziauddin Sardar, whose focus is

Muslim Thought. In addition to the people on this list, some futurists focus on human resources, Black culture, Hispanic culture, and I, who focus on the future of DEI and all of its associated practices. And finally, there are business leaders who are futurists in their industries. Futurists in each of these areas look for emerging trends that may seem small in the present but have the potential to turn into major events that disrupt the area of their interest. We call these signs of future trends, signals. Signals could be anything. They could be a geopolitical event, a new technology development, a demographic change, or several other things. A tropical disturbance in the Gulf of Mexico is an example of a signal.

The second thing we do as futurists is to explore potential outcomes. To illustrate this, let's use a simple example. Say you own a lumber yard in Florida. You hear the news that a tropical disturbance is threatening to become a hurricane. This process can take hours or days. Next, you hear that it's on the move and Florida is on its potential path. At this point, it could make landfall as a category five killer or a tropical storm almost anywhere across the state. As you watch the storm, you consider two extreme outcomes. Either A, this is a catastrophe, and you need to prepare; or B, this is a huge opportunity for your lumbar business. People will need wood to board up their homes and protect their possessions. Some situations can yield more than two potential outcomes. Whether it's two, ten, or more, the futurist wants to explore all possibilities.

And finally, the third thing we need to do as futurists is to consider actions that you and others can take to eliminate or minimize potential negative outcomes and amplify and get the most out of potential positive outcomes. So, continuing with our Floridian lumberyard owner, here are some of his considerations. Stock up on wood to sell to clients preparing for the storm. Set aside some wood to board up his home and business to protect his possessions. Prepare bags with supplies and have an exit strategy in the event he and his family need to evacuate.

And that, in a nutshell, is what we futurists do. Now admittedly, while detailed and accurate, the above description of what futurists do may not be the easiest to remember and apply regularly. The good news is that there is a much simpler formula published back in 1948 by an author named Dale Carnegie.

Dale Carnegie was born on November 24, 1888, on a farm in Missouri. As a teenager, Carnegie developed an interest in public speaking. According to his own story, when he was sixteen, he would get up at 3 am so he could feed the pigs and milk the cows before going to school, where he'd joined the debate team. Carnegie became an accomplished lecturer and writer who started a training business that's still operating today. Nevertheless, Carnegie once said of himself that he "was one of the unhappiest lads in New York." He said he made himself sick with worry about his position in life. It was those feelings of worry about his future that inspired Carnegie to write one of his most notable books, at the age of sixty, in 1948. The book is titled *How to Stop Worrying and Start Living.* In that book, he lays out a simple question and answer process you can use to manage your future. It's extremely easy to use. You can use it to manage your personal life, career, and to become a more effective futurist ERG or DEI leader.

It all boils down to four simple questions: First, consider the situation in front of you and ask yourself, what is the worst that can happen? After you answer that, ask yourself what can I do to address this outcome if I can't prevent it? Next, ask, what can I do to make it less likely to happen, or to eliminate that negative outcome? Finally ask, what positive thing might come out of this and how can I get the most out of it?

So, let's go back to our Floridian lumberyard owner and walk through the questions with him. Sitting in his store on a sunny day in the eighties, he sees the news on television of a tropical disturbance threatening to become a hurricane. He gets a little rush of anxiety. He pulls out a piece of paper, and writes out the following questions, and responses: what is the worst that can happen? The storm can hit me directly and destroy my home and business. What can I do to address this outcome if I can't prevent it? Make sure my flood and severe weather insurance policies are up to date and on hand. Also, prepare to board up my home and business, and possibly evacuate. What can I do to make it less likely to happen or to eliminate that negative outcome? Make sure I have materials to board up my home and business. What positive thing might come out of this and how can I get the most out of it? I can sell a lot of lumber to people who want to board up and protect their homes and businesses. To that end, let me increase my lumber inventory. And voila! Done and dusted. He's got a plan.

You can use this simple four-question process to come up with a strategy for any future challenge. Just copy the four questions into a note on your smartphone or an index card you keep handy. All you need now are two more things. One, you need to recognize and look for signals. Two, you need to have the mechanism in place to communicate and respond to those signals in a timely manner. The first of these, we will cover in the next chapter where we will look at several signals. The second of these two components is the topic of the final segment of this chapter.

What Do You Need to Put in Place to Respond Effectively to Future Signals?

In 2019, an almost five-year-old case against the Domino's Pizza chain was finally settled in favor of the plaintiff. The Plaintiff was Guillermo Robles. Robles claimed that he could not order his pizza the same as a sighted person despite using screen-reading software. He claimed that Dominos had violated his Americans with Disability Act (ADA) rights. The case arguments went back and forth as the lawyers battled it out. It was judged and appealed for the next four years until the Supreme Court refused to hear Domino's last appeal and put an end to the case. The total cost in dollars is not disclosed, but it must have been in the millions. Think about it, almost five years of litigation. The loser, Domino's, had to pay the winners legal fees along with damages. They also had to fix the accessibility issues on their website. Then there is the reputational cost. Wouldn't it have been cheaper and more productive to put the money into making the website accessible to the blind before this bruhaha and selling pizza to blind people? According to one statistic, 4.4 million people use screen readers. Let's assume that twenty-five percent of them would like to order a pizza online. (I think that is a super-conservative estimate because I love pizza and according to stats so do ninety-eight percent of Americans). Now, let's assume they all buy the cheapest small hand-tossed pizza. (Again, I'm being super-conservative because we always go with the large pie and lots of toppings). That small pie lists for $5.99. And to complete our example, let's say each of these 1.1 million people bought a Domino's pizza once a month for 4 years (For context, surveys say that American Pizza eaters have forty-pies a year). Finally, let's consider that pizza delivery market stats say Dominos has twenty-one-point three percent of the market share). Okay, let's do some simple math. That works out to $92,667,696.00 in pizza sales over those four litigious years. That sounds a lot better than paying for a losing lawsuit.

Here's how Domino's talks about their company to would-be job seekers on their website: "We are a company built on innovative solutions and a belief that we are never done getting better, we embrace change and the potential it unlocks for everyone." It goes on to say, "We are focused on developing an inclusive culture, with dignity and respect for all, where team members can grow, thrive, and bring their best selves to work every day. The diversity of our workforce is what helps to make us an enduring brand, where we can grow and thrive together." I believe they mean these words. I also think they hire a broad swath of diversity, which includes people with disabilities. So, what happened? Why couldn't those diverse and inclusive voices have gotten the ear of the leaders making the decisions that led to pursuing a five-year-long losing lawsuit, with market opportunity losses to boot? I never worked for this company or spoke to an insider. This is just pure speculation. But if I were to guess, I would say an ineffective communication structure. I believe these business leaders were "flying blind" despite having all the information they needed to make a better decision right under their noses. And they are not alone.

Consider the number of companies out there that hire consultants for millions of dollars to run focus groups on topics such as what their African American or female consumers want. Sitting right there within their walls are a Black ERG and Women's ERG. Can't they provide that input? Of course, they can. But do they even know that their company is conducting this study? Probably not. This weakness in the communication structures between the various employees, ERGs, other internal and external groups, is what makes it almost impossible for companies to live up to their dreams of becoming more agile and responsive. The typical solution of putting together the senior leaders to come up with solutions in the absence of the perspectives of an increasingly diverse team in a complex and fast-moving workforce/workplace, and marketplace, does not work. It produces bad, or at best, short-sighted decisions. It's also not good for you as an ERG or DEI leader. So, in the absence of a well-integrated communications system like the one at Froedtert, what can you do as an ERG leader? There are two simple steps you can take.

First, make sure you have a well-connected executive sponsor. A well-connected executive sponsor has access to the top of your company. Ideally, the CEO. They are also connected to external business stakeholders who are part of the community you focus on. If your current executive sponsor does not meet that criterion, go out and find another one. No rule says you can only have one executive sponsor. Just make sure at least one of your sponsors can communicate your perspectives to leadership and make you aware of issues and opportunities leadership is facing.

Second, use some of your meetings to collect the concerns, desires, and perspectives of your members. As noted by Gavin from Froedtert, this is a simple but powerful way to find out what your community is hearing and what they're seeking. You and your fellow group leaders should have a finger on the pulse of your ERG. This is easier to do than ever, even in between meetings. As noted by Parr, her group at Hiscox does it using available technologies, like WhatsApp and Yammer.

Of course, it would be ideal if your organization built a more tightly integrated system of communication across the entire enterprise. That would enable your group and other ERGs to simply plug in. It would also provide your company with a great deal of data that would help make them more agile. But in the absence of this larger solution, you can quickly connect yourself, your community, and your senior leadership just by following the two steps outlined above.

So, let's quickly summarize the highlights from this chapter:

1. As ERG and DEI leaders, you need to be aware of unfolding events so that you can avoid obstacles and pounce on opportunities.
2. That means you need to become a futurist. This doesn't mean that you become accurate predictors of the future. It means you

need to become good at seeing signals of change that bring obstacles and opportunities and creating strategies to get the best results.

3. You can use a simple four-question approach to improve your skills as a future strategist.
4. Like a major league baseball hitter's eye-to-brain-to arms, you need a superior communication system. If your company has one, plug in. If it doesn't, you can easily build one for your ERG in two steps.

Now as promised, in the next chapter we're going to look at all the signals of what's to come in the next one to ten years. Happy future trails!

Chapter Bibliography

1. s.l. : National Science & Technology Medals Foundation, 2009. https://nationalmedals.org/laureate/steven-sasson/.
2. Steve Sasson, Digital Camera Inventor. s.l. : Kodak, 2008.
3. Morgan, Jacob. The Future Leader. s.l. : Wiley, 2020.
4. Quinton, Sean. Don't Blink: The science of a 100mph fastball. s.l. : The Seattle Times, 2017.
5. Abbatine, Tony Dr. Laby, Daniel M., M.D. Dr. Kirschen, David G. Ph.D., OD. Scope and Rope: A Visual Profile of Major League Hitters. https://www.baseballamerica.com/stories/scope-and-rope-a-visual-profile-of-major-league-hitters/.
6. Herrman, John. s.l. : New York Times, 2021. https://www.nytimes.com/2021/11/23/business/dealbook/futurology-predictions.html.

CHAPTER 4
A Peek into Our Future

In times of change, learners inherit the earth; while the learned find themselves beautifully equipped to deal with a world that no longer exists.
*– **Eric Hoffer***

On March 11, 2020, I was back from St Kitts in New York City. I was still acclimating to the shift from a tropical climate to the last gasps of winter in New York. The weather was an overcast 52 degrees. I was taping a panel for an episode of the ERG PowerTalk podcast, which I usually look forward to and enjoy. But that day my anxiety level was starting to dial up. Earlier that week, my gym had sent out a note announcing they would be closed, and several colleagues had told me they would now be working from home. To put a cap on this steady drumbeat of alarm, that day Tedros Adhanom Ghebreyesus, director-general of the World Health Organization declared COVID-19 a pandemic. At a briefing in Geneva, he said he was "deeply concerned by the alarming levels of spread and severity." Two days later March 13, 2020, the United States followed suit. These were days of reckoning. COVID-19 wasn't a simple variation of the flu. It was also slightly before and around this time that the first signal of an upcoming shift in the future that would impact organizations and ERGs showed up.

Right before the pandemic, a tiny six percent of the American workforce was working remotely. According to a McKinsey study from 2009 to 2019, that number had grown only two percentage points from four percent. So, while many companies, like IBM, were experimenting with working from home all the way back in the 1980s, progress was slow. Even after decades of progress in technology and remote meeting platforms, ninety-four percent of the workforce still went to an employee-owned workplace. Of those ninety-four percent, about ten-point eight percent worked evening shifts. Another six-point five percent worked night shifts. And finally, we had two-point-five percent of workers on rotating shifts that alternate between day and night. That means seventy-four-point two percent of the workforce, close to three quarters, work together with their colleagues in the same company-owned building, at the same time every day. But in 2020, the pandemic created a situation where almost everything in the economy that was possible to do remotely, became remote work overnight [(1)].

It's estimated that about thirty-five percent of the workforce went into remote work. Zooming became a verb and watercoolers in company-owned buildings around the country were deserted. After vaccines became available and the dust started to settle, a whooping twenty-four- percent of the workforce remained remote. This happened even in the face of employer pressure to corral people back into company-owned buildings. In fact, some people would rather quit their jobs than go back to the old workplace. The reasons for this resistance are varied but strong. The bottom line is that a large block of the workforce is refusing to go back to pre-pandemic business-as-usual. In addition to this, in the abundance of caution, many organizations have limited the number of people that can be in a building at the same time. This has increased the number of people working shifts or coming on separate days to the same building.

The outcome of all this has been the redistribution of people across, what I call, the four dimensions of the workplace. These four dimensions have been with us for a long time. Some have been full of employees, while others were almost completely empty. One of them appeared in the 1990s when email was first introduced. Here's a quick look at each of these workplace dimensions.

The first dimension of the workplace is the same place at the same time. This is where seventy-four-point two percent of the workforce found themselves before COVID-19. Whether to an office or factory, these people commuted to a location where they worked for the most part with other colleagues. They might make phone calls to people outside or go out to meet clients for lunch, but for the most part, their corporate building was their workplace. That's also where you held your ERG and DEI meetings in conference rooms or celebrated cultural history months.

The second dimension of the workplace is a different place at the same time. Here's where our remote workers resided. Up to 2019, these were the six percent that were often forgotten. Many had little interaction with their company, except with their immediate supervisor and people working on a shared project. Many felt they were being passed over for promotions in favor of those colleagues who got more "facetime." Very few, if any, were part of any ERGs or attended their events.

The third dimension of the workplace is the same place at a different time. This is where pre-COVID, we had nineteen-point nine percent of the workforce. (Evening shifts plus night shifts plus rotating shifts). Like their remote cousins, this group was usually left out of events enjoyed by the seventy-four-point two percent.

And the fourth and final dimension of the workplace is a different time from a different place. This one contains people who use products like email and shared docs to work with colleagues without having to be in the same place or working at the same time.

These Work Dimensions Are Not New, But the Potential Redistribution of People is New

As noted earlier, none of the workplace dimensions are new. The signal we are seeing is not in their presence. The signal is in the redistribution of people across them and what that means for DEI efforts and ERGs. The first signal of change impacting ERGs and DEI is that fewer people are working in the same place at the same time, and those people are moving into the other three workplace dimensions. For example, twenty-four percent remain in the remote work category of the same time, but different place. According to McKinsey an estimated twenty-nine percent of work in the United States could be done remotely with no productivity loss, and an additional ten percent could be done remotely if needed. Translation: There is an opportunity for this dimension of the workplace to continue to grow using current tools and resources. That could continue to take more people out of the traditional same place same time at the company building category.

Likewise, we've seen growth in the same place at a different time dimension that once contained only nineteen-point-nine percent of the workforce. We don't have an exact number here in terms of growth, but as businesses limit their building occupancy capacity out of caution, one way they do it is by having workers come in on different days or times. At the time I am writing this, virologists are examining the COVID19 variant, Omicron, which they fear may be able to defeat the current vaccines. That indicates that we may be entering an era where some type of gathering-size-controls will need to become a more regular feature of life. For corporations, which might mean more shift workers.

And finally, we have a steady increase in people working across countries and time zones. That seems to indicate that the different time and different place dimension is poised to expand as well. In fact, companies, like Loom, are betting hundreds of millions of dollars on this dimension's projected growth. In the past, people working at different times from different places had far fewer tools than their colleagues working in one of the other three workplace dimensions. They could only email, send text messages, or share Google docs. Loom means to change that by becoming the new "email on camera." Loom is basically a platform that enables users to record videos for work that can be easily shared quickly. These videos are not just meeting recordings. They enable users to share their screen, and visually and orally communicate with one or more video recipients and discussion participants. The company, which was founded six years ago by Joe Thomas, Vinay Hiremath, and Shahed Khan, is growing fast. At the time of this writing, Loom has already onboarded fourteen million-plus users, raised $160 million, and hosted 100 million-plus sessions.

So, let's pause here and tally these signals:

- Twenty-four percent of the workforce remains remote, and experts assess that up to thirty-nine percent of the workforce can work remotely.

- □ Continuous variations of COVID are forcing organizations to limit gathering sizes from their former pre-pandemic levels.
- □ Innovators and investors are placing big bets on tools that support people working from different places at different times.

What does that mean for the former dominant dimension of the workplace, same place at the same time? I think means that it will be lucky if it can hold at least thirty percent of the workforce over the next decade. And this, in turn, means that all your old DEI ERG practices need to be revisited and revised for this new world. Why? Because if we don't, we may be serving only the people in the shrinking same place at the same time workplace dimension. Or like Longfield at Dollar General, we might discover how to leverage these changes to extend the number of people we can engage.

The bottom line is that you cannot ignore these signals. You need strategies that consider and prepare for all the possible outcomes. And you need to come up with it fast because as this fast ball closes the distance, the pitcher is already winding up for the next one.

What Might be Coming Next?

On October 7, 2019, a pop-up café opened for visitors in Otemachi, Japan. The spacious room was filled with blond wooden tables, like those long tables we often see in a local Starbucks. The place was teaming with people seated or standing waiting to be seated. This café was part of a project sponsored by a company called OryLab Inc. Guests were there to be served coffee and tea and chat with their servers. Except, none of their servers were in the building.

All of the servers in this lab café' are bedridden patients with amyotrophic lateral sclerosis (ALS) or spinal muscular atrophy (SMA). So how do these servers take orders, bring drinks and chat with their guests? Through avatar robots, designed by OryLab. These Robots are not controlled by AI. Instead, the robots are connected via Wi-Fi to the Internet and are managed by bedridden operators known as "pilots." In this experiment, they used 30 pilots, including a sixteen-year-old high-school girl, who is bedridden, in a special school in Fukuoka, Japan, about an hour away from the café.

One of these "pilots" runs a robot affixed to each table that takes the guests' orders once they are seated. Other pilots then operate other robots that bring the drinks to the tables and chat with guests. Visitors can have the same type of conversation with the pilots through the robot avatars as they would if they were physically in front of each other. The purpose of the experimental café in Otemachi was to learn and refine the process and the experience for pilots and guests. It's also there to help the creators to discover new applications. According to the Co-founder & CEO of OryLab, Kentaro, Yoshifuji, a thirty-year-old young man sporting shoulder-length dark hair, the purpose of this effort is to enable people who would otherwise be unable to work, to find gainful employment in a variety of fields beyond serving in a coffee shop. Yoshifuji was inspired to take on this mission after finding himself bedridden in a hospital for the better part of three years, between the age of ten and fourteen. I agree with him and think we can all see this can do all that and much more [(2)]. Think for example warehouse work, receptionist, etc.

Since that experiment, things have moved quickly. Less than two years after the 2019 experiment, on June 22, 2021, Tokyo officially opened a café run by robots, operated by bedridden human pilots. Videos and news reports indicate that the shop is a big hit. Unlike robotic experiments in the United States that aim to replace humans completely with machines, these human-robot approaches appear to be more successful. They also open a new door for who can work on what and from where.

If you can be a restaurant server using a robotic avatar from a bed across town over the Internet, why can't you do it from another State or Country? So not only does this technology expand work opportunities to millions of people who are disabled, but also increases the kinds of jobs that can be done remotely and the potential distance from which these jobs can be performed. How might that impact the flow of people across the four dimensions of the workplace? Also, how might it have an impact on what organizations consider their available workforce pool? And this is just one of two other forces that might have a big impact on your ERGs and your DEI workforce, workplace, and marketplace efforts.

Why Stop at Four Dimensions?

As if the redistribution of people across a four-dimensional workplace were not enough, now we are seeing the emergence of what we can call the fifth dimension. For those of you that weren't geeky comic book readers of the last century like me, the fifth dimension might be a new term. The term fifth dimension was coined by the German mathematician, Theodor Kaluza and Swedish physicist, Oskar Klein, in the early twentieth century, to describe a place where electromagnetism and gravity unify. That's not, however, where I first heard of it. I first heard of the fifth dimension as the place Superman's magical nemesis, Mister Mxyzptlk (pronounced mix-ee-yez-pit-lik) came from. But I digress since neither of these is the fifth dimension we're talking about.

The fifth dimension we're talking about here was created by humans. It was in the making for a long time. It's literally a collection of different technologies, such as virtual reality and augmented reality tools connected via the Internet. For a while, it had no name. The name of this new dimension came about as the result of a new portmanteau created by combining the Greek word for many, *meta*, with the Latin word for together, *universum*, in the early1990s. This new dimension for activity was called the metaverse. Even after it got its name, it remained somewhat in the background, until Facebook, who changed its name to Meta, brought it center stage to the masses in 2021. That year, as part of their name change announcement, the company released a video of Mark Zuckerberg, Co-founder, and CEO of Meta (formally Facebook, Inc), and others interacting within this virtual metaverse world. It didn't take a lot of imagination to visualize people collaborating, working, and meeting in this metaverse from places all around the world. Combine this with all the instant translation and AI voice generation tools coming out and it's not hard to imagine people from all over the world, who use different languages, meeting with colleagues, and having a robust dialogue understood by all in the metaverse. So now we have a fifth dimension added to our workplace model. Okay, you might think, but it will be a while before this new dimension starts to fill up with people. Perhaps not as long as you think. Just look at the long line of people waiting to get in.

There are about four point eight million of them. Another seventeen million people, according to research, would love to join them [(3)]. They're generally in their forties and have been living on the road for about ten years. Although the oldest of them is seventy-two years old. They come from all over the world, but primarily they are Americans, Portuguese, Germans, and Brazilians. They love freedom and do not want to work in a business-owned building. Their educational credentials vary from Ph.D. and MD to non-degreed people who are self-taught. They live all over the world in apartments, guesthouses, BnBs, hostels, or hotels. You can find them in places as far apart as Mexico and Thailand, and everything in between, including the Caribbean, Middle East, and all over Eastern and Western Europe. They are called digital nomads and twenty-four regions in the world offer them digital nomad visas [(4)]. These visas are travel authorizations that legalize the status of workers on the move. Like tourist visas, they are easy to obtain. They allow long stays and allow its holder to work during their stay in the country, provided they do so independently and remotely. And an increasing number of countries are jumping on board this trend and offering their visitors digital work visas. The metaverse was made for these people who do not want to be tethered to a location close to their work.

So, let's stop here to review and add these signals to our growing list:

- □ We now have a growing number of technologies that enable people to perform work that used to require a physical presence, remotely.
- □ The metaverse is developing into the fifth dimension of life where people can interact in an almost in-person way across distances vast and small.
- □ There are about four point eight million digital nomads (with seventeen million more people who would like to join them waiting in the wings), who can swell in rank from knowledge

workers to physical workers with meetings in the metaverse almost instantly.

But you might think, "well, these digital nomads tend to be independent workers, so they won't impact my DEI or ERGs. We focus on employees and ERGs are for employees." Well, that is precisely what the next set of signals is going to invite you to revisit.

The New Company Workforce

In the 1980s, a new element was noticed in the American labor force. Through the years, that new element continued to grow and become more complex. By 1999, about five point six million people were in this workforce category. At the time, it represented a mere four-point three percent of the US workforce. According to a recent US Government Accountability report, this element now represents forty percent of the entire workforce [5]. In 1985, Audrey Freedman, a Labor Economist coined the term "contingent work," to describe the activities of these new members of the workforce.

Before the rise of this contingent workforce, if you ran into someone in your company building, you could almost safely bet that they were another employee. Today, you have a sixty to forty chance of being right or wrong. What's more, by 2050, those same reports project that this contingent workforce will reach fifty percent. So, who exactly are these new members of this workforce group? Generally, contingent workers fall into one of three sub-categories.

The first contingent worker category is the temporary worker. The staffing industry in the United States began after World War II. In the early days of this practice, it involved small agencies in urban areas employing housewives for part-time work as office workers. Over the years employers were attracted to the advantages of having workers who could be hired and fired on short notice. These workers were also exempt from paperwork and regulatory requirements. This resulted in a steady increase in the use of temporary workers. By the beginning of the new millennium, there were over three point five million temporary workers in the United States [6]. According to labor forecasters, temporary employment in the U.S. is projected to grow faster at eight-point-five percent than jobs that are expected to only grow at only six percent through the year 2025 (7).

The second contingent worker category is the freelance contractor. Our earliest written reference to the word "freelance" comes from Sir Walter Scott's novel, *Ivanhoe*, published in1820. In this book, a lord character refers to his paid army of "free lancers." He was referring to a medieval mercenary who would fight for whichever nation or person paid them the most. Today, a freelance worker refers to someone self-employed, that works for others, without long-term commitments to any single employer. Another common term used to refer to this group is independent contractors. The number of people freelancing jumped from twenty-eight percent of the workforce in 2019 to thirty-six percent in 2020, according to a study by Upwork, a leading online freelance talent agency. Many of these workers don't want to go back into full-time employment (8).

The third contingent worker category is the member of a strategic ally's team that is temporarily on loan or working on a collaborative project between the corporate partners. Many large and small companies today enter a strategic alliance to expand into a new market, improve product lines, or develop an edge over a competitor. Fifty-seven percent of companies today use strategic partners to acquire new customers. More than two thousand strategic alliances are formed each year with that number growing by fifteen percent each year (9). Members of a strategic alliance often share employees over long and short-term projects. One example of this type of alliance can be seen in the Siemens, Disney, Marvel Alliance.

As early as 1911, Siemens had begun the development of electrical hearing aids. By 1959, Siemens had produced the world's first behind-the-ear hearing aid and in 1966, they released the first in-the-ear hearing aid. Some years ago, Siemens was looking for ways to convince deaf children to use their hearing aids. Most kids didn't think it was cool to wear a hearing aid. This was a marketing challenge. Siemens had a marketing team, but that team did not have experience with children. Instead of hiring new marketing team members, Siemens turned to their strategic partners over at Disney who had just acquired Marvel Entertainment. Disney certainly had team members experienced with marketing to children and so did Marvel.

One of the results of this collaboration was the creation of a new superhero called Blue Ear. Blue Ear is a superhero whose distinctive listening device gives him supersonic hearing. This enables him to hear cries for help. It also makes wearing a hearing aid cool for kids like Anthony Smith of New Hampshire [(10)]. This is just one of many such collaborations that exist today and more seem to be coming onto the horizon.

So how might this transformation of the workforce impact your DEI and ERG efforts? Well, like most organizational people-practices, ERGs, as their very name tells us, are rooted in the company employee model. If companies have fewer employees and more contingent workers, this will cut deeply into the number of people covered by your workforce and workplace efforts. Unless you and your organization come up with new strategies.

Let's pause again here to update our list of signals:

- □ In addition to a redistribution of the workforce across the old four dimensions of the workplace and a new one being added, the percentage of employees in our companies is giving way to a new growing contingent workforce.
- □ We still don't know which of the subcategories of this new contingent workforce will dominate the landscape in a few years, but they are collectively growing faster than the employee category.
- □ Current company practices and many state laws make it difficult for DEI and ERGs to include non-employees.

Okay, so now we've built quite a future picture of change loaded with possibilities. But we need to consider one more element. This is an element that adds yet another component to the evolving workforce. A non-human element that promises to be another big game-changer.

The Thinking Machine

In 1984, like millions of other moviegoers, I sat in a packed theater and watched a robot, played by Arnold Schwarzenegger, doggedly pursue and try to kill a young woman, played by Linda Hamilton. The plot was simple and dark. The robot was sent from the year 2029 by an artificial intelligence (AI) called Skynet. Its mission was to prevent the birth of a man named John Conner. In the future, Conner defeats Skynet and saves mankind from extinction. The AI's strategy to turn the tables was simple. Send one of its killers to the past and murder Conner's mother before he's born. The movie was dark and apocalyptic. And it mirrored the views about AI of another movie I'd recently seen on television, 2001: A Space Odyssey. In this film, another AI, called HAL, goes rogue and kills crew members of a spaceship while holding a calm but scary dialogue with a scientist named Dave. I think all of us who watched these movies left them feeling a bit paranoid about AIs.

Flash forward to the present where I live in a home like the one occupied by millions of people. As I work in my home office in the early morning, I hear the three short tones that tell me "Rosie," our AI-controlled vacuum robot is about to clean our floors. Meanwhile, I get short useful responses to my spot research questions from my Amazon Echo. I can reach our Echo through one of many devices around my house or the Fitbit I wear on my right wrist. I can, if I want, redirect the robot vacuum through the Fitbit since they are all linked to the Amazon Echo. Later, I drive to Starbucks to pick up a coffee in my car that automatically nudges me into my lane if the onboard AI detects that I am making a lane change I did not signal. Later that day I peruse Amazon for a new book, and I'm met with a boatload of recommendations by the sites AI based on my previous purchases. Likewise, when I settle down to watch a movie on Netflix in the evening, I'm greeted by another AI's recommendations based on what we've watched in the past. I could go on, but I think this is enough to make the point. Despite earlier apprehension brought on by dystopian movies, many of us have been slowly but steadily surrounded by AI-powered tools. And this is not just something happening in our personal lives. Organizations today are rapidly putting AI into everything they do.

In the late nineteenth century and into the early twentieth century, everything in the world was being electrified. In 1872 the electric ticker tape printer was born. Some years later in 1907's, we got the electric vacuum cleaner. A little over a decade after that, we got the electric washing machine in 1923. A century later, everything is being made intelligent. This is especially true when it comes to how organizations are managing their workforces. There are AI programs that scan resumes and determine who should get on the hiring manager's short list. There are AI-powered chatbots that can conduct initial interviews. A chatbot is a software application that conducts an online conversation via text or text-to-speech with a person. Some are so good that you may not realize you are communicating with a machine. Other programs instantly determine the new recruit's salary range based on several pieces of collected and stored data. And then some other AIs can monitor employee communications and determine who's at risk of leaving the organization or disengaged with their work.

Some AIs monitor and guide your relationships with your organization's clients. For example, some AIs guide the course of patient treatment in healthcare organizations. Some AIs make sentencing recommendations to court judges. And there are AIs in banks and other credit-granting institutions that determine who should get and who should not get a loan. Again, I can go on, but I think you get the point. AI is embedded in almost every single aspect of the workforce relationship with the organization. Many decisions that were made by humans in the past are today made by AIs.

AI offers organizations speed and savings. For example, while a good human recruiter can scan one resume in six seconds, a decent AI can review six hundred in one second. Also, while a good human recruiter can hold eight thirty-minute candidate prescreening interviews and complete their shortlist for a hiring manager in say five hours, a chatbot can do all eight interviews simultaneously and produce the shortlist mere seconds later. It can take HR hours of scouring through occupational manuals online to come up with a salary range that an AI can produce in seconds. Numbers like that tell us that more organizations will be jumping on the AI bandwagon. That all sounds great, but there is a downside that DEI and ERG leaders need to consider with the seemingly all-knowing, God-like programs.

The Gods Are Flawed But No One Seems to Know It

About two years ago, I was approached by a super-excited colleague. Let's call him Richard. That's not his real name. Richard wanted me to partner with him and a company that had produced an AI-powered tool that would help project managers build their pool of project resources. My role would be to support the adoption of this tool throughout the DEI community. "This tool will democratize the process of selecting people to work on projects and will create greater access and inclusion," Richard gushed. What he was referring to was ending the current cliquish way that project managers selected people for their projects based only on the small circle of people they know and trust. By having everyone's qualifications placed into a database without reference to gender, race, ethnicity, etc., Richard and his company partners felt this would make the entire process fairer and more equitable. I didn't agree. I asked Richard how users of the program would detect, flag, and address bias. He said that no action was needed since the program did not collect any information about gender, race, or other demographic particulars. I pushed on and asked, what factors users were entering into the program to indicate that a person has certain useful skills or talents? Richard said it was just pure data about skills and talent. I stopped pushing and declined to join him and the company to support the project.

The presence of this blind spot about the potential flaws in AI that can lead to bias in the workplace shocked me so much, I decided to launch a study into the matter. In the 2020 CDO PowerCircle survey that went out to HR leaders, one of the questions I included was the following: What impact will AI have on workplace inclusion through the elimination of bias? The response choices included were the following: (a) Will automatically increase inclusion, (b) Will decrease inclusion, or (c) Note sure. To my shock over sixty-three percent of HR leaders believed that the introduction of AI would automatically increase workplace inclusion. What's more, a full seventy percent of them believed it would automatically increase marketplace inclusion. Nothing could be farther from what AI experts know and tell us. But the verdict is in. The AI Gods had flaws that are invisible to many of the most senior HR gatekeepers.

To understand those "flaws" that result in bias and how they enter these AI tools, we need to first get a bit of an understanding of how these tools come into being and how they work. "Machine learning happens the same way toddlers learn language, through exposure to training data," according to Amin Venjara, General Manager of Data Solutions at ADP. As explained by Venjara, an expert in machine learning and analytics, AI programs are developed by other programs that build the AI using training data. Here's an example. Suppose I want to develop a program that helps a company hire the best candidates. We currently have ten thousand records of past hires and the history of their performance in the company. We consider a successful hire, someone who stayed with the company for more than ten years, maintained and exceeded expected performance ratings throughout their career with us, and got promoted to more senior levels three times during their time with us. We now take five thousand resumes and label each one as either a success or failure. Successes are the resumes of people who under our set conditions are considered to have succeeded. Failures are people who failed to meet our conditions for success. Next, we feed these resumes to a program that reads them and looks for commonalities between the successes and commonalities between the failures. Using this "training data," the program generates another program designed to look for the elements that it has identified are most common to the successful people's resumes. That program is your resume screening AI. Before it's put to work on candidate resumes, the new program is tested. In this case, the test consists of feeding it the other five thousand resumes from the historical database. The new AI, unlike the other program that built the AI, is not told who succeeded or failed. If the new AI tool accurately categorizes a high percentage of the successes and failures correctly, then it's deemed ready to be used to screen new candidate resumes. And, essentially, some form of this development of a program by a program using historical data for training, followed by testing of the newly generated program using more historical data is the process via which many AIs are created.

Many of the creators of these tools take several measures to avoid bias getting into these systems. For example, they don't include names, gender, or race and ethnicity information in the training and testing data. Nevertheless, biases do creep into all AI tools. Here's a classic example involving eCommerce giant Amazon.

Since 2014, Amazon's engineers had worked on an AI recruitment tool to help the company find top candidates buried in mountains of resumes. By the beginning of 2017 Amazon abandoned the project. Why? Because they discovered that their AI was biased against female candidates, and they could not find a way to fix the problem. It turns out that the AI was developed and trained using ten years of Amazon's resume data. Like most technology companies, Amazon historically hired and promoted primarily men. This parade of successful male hires is what the AI saw in the training data. And based on this, the AI concluded that men were a better match for the company. Despite all the engineer's efforts to mask gender and make the system less biased, the AI would still find ways to give preferential treatment to men and reject female applicants. For example, it would detect things like "Captain of Women's Tennis Club," and sideline a candidate. In the end, the company pulled the plug and scrapped the effort [(11)].

Similar biases have been found in other tools. For example, take an AI system, called COMPASS, used by judges in courtrooms across America in forty-six States. COMPASS is supposed to predict the likelihood of a defendant committing future crimes and based on that make sentencing recommendations to the judge. In 2016 ProPublica reported that Black defendants were labeled as "high-risk" at twice the rate as White defendants. The reason for the bias was attributed in part to the historical data used to train the AI, which was laced with our history of judicial biases [(12)]. Another example is found in a healthcare risk assessment AI used to determine the level of care needed for about two hundred million Americans. According to a study led by Ziad Obermeyer, an assistant professor of health policy at the University of California, Berkeley, Black patients lost out on badly needed critical care because the AI determined health needs based on how much people paid for healthcare in the past [(13)].

In each of these cases, the problem was with the proxy used by the system. A proxy is basically a factor that is used to represent something else. So, for example, a college degree is a form of proxy often used to determine the presence of education and intelligence. When we ask a computer system to generate an AI that determines who we should hire what we call a "high performer," we are asking the system to find the common proxy factors across all the successful examples we provide and then use those to predict what resume belongs to someone like those successful examples. Since our historical data is loaded with proxies based on our assumptions about who will be successful that influence us consciously and unconsciously, these will always find their way in through training examples. In the AIs blind and deaf data-driven world, it will take each of these factors and include them in its final formula for finding "winners." Take that and the blind spots and biases of programmers and the people who buy these tools and you can see how we end up with so many cases of machine bias that gets past the radar of HR, law enforcement, healthcare, and just about everyone.

That's why I was pressing my colleague so hard on the matter of the project assignment AI he was pushing. I wanted to know how it was trained and what proxies it might be using that could sideline people. For example, say the project manager wanted the AI to find programmers for a project. Based on the training data, the AI might be looking for a college degree as a proxy for having the right programming skill level. Well according to statistics on programmers, twenty-seven percent don't hold a degree. So that automatically would sideline this non-degreed group, Let's further add to our example that the training data favored Ivy league school degrees. Most likely, people that come from families that can afford prestigious schools have these Ivy league school degrees. That will result in further sidelining of some candidates. Note here that most programmers, eighty-six percent, degreed or not, cite that one of the ways they learn their craft is through teaching themselves by using tools on their own. In other words, their degree did not make them better programmers. Logically, we know that these degrees often represent the financial status of the parents more than the skill and talent capabilities of the candidates. But to the AI this Ivy league degree is an important proxy for high qualifications. Notice, that the AI has not been directly trained to prefer white males. But I will bet you that a large portion of the candidates selected for the programmer assignment by an AI looking for people with an Ivy league advanced degree will be white men.

My concern with my colleague and the company was not that they could not prove that their AI tool was perfect. My concern was with their lack of awareness, intentional or unintentional, of the potential biases in their tools. Let me just say as an extension of what my good friend and fellow author Howard Ross likes to say: "I'm biased, you're biased, we're all biased," and to that, I will add all our AI tools are biased too.

Now before we close this topic, let's just clarify one thing. AI is not evil. It is not anti-diversity, equity, and inclusion. In fact, AI can be supportive of your ERG and DEI efforts. For example, there's a new AI tool that helps users prepare and rehearse for better and more inclusive speeches. Now there's a tool DEI and ERG leaders can use to train themselves and managers to be more inclusive speakers without an audience. You can also work with AI development and installation teams to make many of the HR tools they use more equitable and inclusive. (More on that in a future chapter). The important point to note here is that you should not shy away from challenging these tools when you detect biases or using them to improve inclusion and equity. They are simply another element of the future that you need to factor into your strategy as a futurist who wants to drive more inclusion and equity.

Getting Your Arms Around the Big Picture

Okay, let's take our final pause in this chapter to update our list of signals and then wrap up. Let's begin by reviewing the first nine signals and then adding the final three:

- □ Twenty-four percent of the workforce remains remote post-pandemic, and expert assessments are that up to thirty-nine percent of the workforce can work remotely.
- □ Continuous variations of COVID are forcing organizations to limit gathering sizes from their former pre-pandemic levels.
- □ Innovators and investors are placing big bets on tools that support people working from different places at different times.
- □ We now have a growing number of technologies that enable people to perform work that used to require a physical presence remotely.

- The metaverse is developing into the fifth dimension of life where people can interact in an almost in-person way across distances vast and small.
- There are about four point eight million digital nomads (with seventeen million more people who would like to join them waiting in the wings), who can swell in rank from knowledge workers to physical workers with meetings in the metaverse almost instantly.
- In addition to a redistribution of the workforce across the old four dimensions of the workplace and a new one being added, the percentage of employees in our companies is giving way to a new growing contingent workforce.
- We still don't know which of the subcategories of this new contingent workforce will dominate the landscape in a few years, but they are collectively growing faster than the employee category.
- Current company practices and many state laws make it difficult for DEI efforts and ERG groups to include non-employees, especially in ERG group leadership roles.

And to these we add:

- Artificial intelligence programs are all around us and gradually taking bigger roles in the workforce, workplace, and marketplace decisions. Who companies hire, what they pay them, who they promote, or fire increasingly is driven by AI assessments and recommendations. The same is true about how companies service their clients.
- AI is never bias-free. It's also not always good or bad. It is ultimately what we, its users, make it.
- DEI leaders and ERG leaders and groups that want to drive more inclusion and equity into their workforce, workplace, and marketplace cannot just stand on the sidelines when it comes to AI.

That is a boatload of signals. There are lots of variables and no one can accurately predict how all this will pan out. As futurist leaders, you need to consider and prepare for a full range of outcomes. Ideally, you want to have strategies for minimizing the impact of outcomes you don't want and maximizing the results of outcomes you do want. To start thinking about this, let's use the simple four-question model we covered in chapter three.

1. First, consider the situation in front of you and ask yourself, what is the worst that can happen?
2. After you answer that, ask yourself what can I do to address this outcome if I can't prevent it?
3. Next, ask what can I do to make it less likely or eliminate that negative outcome?
4. Finally ask, what positive thing might come out of this and how can I get the most out of it?

Your responses to these questions can be quite detailed. Ideally, you will compare your responses to those of your colleagues in your group and company. Once you've done this step, you will have an outline of your general future strategy.

Once this is done, you need to focus on making your DEI and ERG efforts nimbler. That's the only way you'll be able to respond to all these rapidly shifting changes in a timely manner. How to make yourself nimbler is the focus of our next two chapters.

Chapter Bibliography

1. Remote Work Before, During, and After the Pandemic. s.l. : NCCI, 2020. https://www.ncci.com/SecureDocuments/QEB/QEB_Q4_2020_RemoteWork.html.
2. Avatar Robot Cafe Dawn Version Beta 2.0. s.l. : Japan Times, 2019. https://www.youtube.com/watch?v=26naiZ7bGlY.
3. Digital Nomads: Leading the Trend for Remote Work. 2018. https://www.mbopartners.com/state-of-independence/research-trends-digital-nomads/.
4. 63 Surprising Digital Nomad Statistics in 2021. s.l. : A Brother Abroad, 2021. https://abrotherabroad.com/digital-nomad-statistics/#WHO-ARE-DIGITAL-NOMADS.
5. Contingent Workforce Landscape: Trends and Strategies. https://www.peoplescout.com/insights/contingent-workforce-landscape-trends/.
6. Temporary Work. s.l. : Wikipedia. https://en.wikipedia.org/wiki/Temporary_work.
7. Temp Employment to Outpace Jobs Through 2025. s.l. : Staffing Monthly Analyst, 2019. https://www2.staffingindustry.com/Editorial/Daily-News/Temp-employment-to-outpace-total-jobs-through-2025-TrueBlue-lists-fastest-growing-temp-occupations-51762.
8. New Upwork Study Finds 36% of the U.S. Workforce Freelance Amid the COVID-19 Pandemic. s.l. : Upwork. https://www.upwork.com/press/releases/new-upwork-study-finds-36-of-the-us-workforce-freelance-amid-the-covid-19-pandemic.

9. 104 stats you never knew about strategic partnerships. s.l.: Breezy, 2020. https://breezy.io/blog/strategic-partnership-stats/#strategic-partnership-statistics.
10. Marvel Comics creates superhero Blue Ear, who uses a hearing aid, to inspire New Hampshire boy. s.l. : Daily News, 2012. https://www.nydailynews.com/news/marvel-comics-creates-superhero-blue-ear-hearing-aid-inspire-new-hampshire-boy-article-1.1085227.
11. Amazon built an AI tool to hire people but had to shut it down because it was discriminating against women. s.l. : Business Insider, 2018. https://www.businessinsider.com/amazon-built-ai-to-hire-people-discriminated-against-women-2018-10.
12. Mesa, Natalia. Can the Criminal Justice Systems Artificial Intelligence Ever Be Truly Fair? s.l. : Massive Science, 2021. https://massivesci.com/articles/machine-learning-compas-racism-policing-fairness/.
13. Vartan, vStarre. Racial Bias Found in a Major Health Care Risk Algorithm. s.l. : Scientific American, 2019. https://www.scientificamerican.com/article/racial-bias-found-in-a-major-health-care-risk-algorithm/.

PART II

Getting Your ERG and DEI Organizations into Shape

Knowing how to look for signs of trends is one key component for succeeding in a rapidly changing world. Another critical factor is making sure your organization, and you are ready to quickly respond to opportunities and challenges. I will offer you twenty tips to prepare you for a faster-moving, more disruptive, digitalized world, in the following two chapters. The first ten are for leaders of ERGs. The ten that follow are for DEI leaders. I recommend you read both, but at a minimum, read the ten most applicable to your role in DEI.

CHAPTER 5

Ten Tips for ERG Leaders

*"Doing your best at this moment puts you in the best place for the next moment." **-Oprah Winfrey***

Before the pandemic and social unrest became headlines in the news, ERG leaders had already faced significant challenges. Here are just a few of the top items I've discovered in my research.

One, running one of these groups places an extra heavy burden on the ERG leader. According to an internal study conducted by an HR software company, called JustWorks, their average ERG leader adds another ten to twenty percent of time spent working on top of their full-time role with the company [(1)]. Let's assume that this ERG leader works thirty-five hours per week for fifty weeks of a year for a total of One thousand-seven-hundred-and-fifty hours per year. That means their ERG work just added one-hundred-and-seventy-five to three-hundred-and-fifty hours of work to their year. That's time taken away from family and friends and other personal activities.

Two, in many cases, ERG leaders find themselves perpetually running a growing list of shadow programs to fill in the gaps that exist in company processes that are not equitable. By the way, these words referring to equity are mine since most ERG leaders, and even some DEI leaders, do not understand or focus on equity. A lack of equity exists in a system when it does not equally support and provide equal opportunity for all the members of a company's workforce. For example, let's say a company's expense reimbursement policy covers all the regular expenses that would be incurred by a man working in sales, like drinks with clients and transportation to and from meetings. But that same policy does not cover any of the other expenses that a woman might incur in sales, such as a babysitter for her toddler. We would say that this system is inequitable in that it does not fully support women the way it helps men. Now let's say a Women in Sales ERG steps in and creates a babysitting network. The women in this group offer to take turns watching each other's toddlers as needed. While this addresses the immediate problem, it does not fix the current inequitable reimbursement system. Unfixed equity issues within recruiting, talent development, and a whole host of other systems often end up being patched by an ever-increasing number of shadow ERG efforts. That creates more work and a burden for ERG leaders and their members.

Three, ERG budgets for all this work and effort are small, and they aren't growing at pace with the work often due to a perceived lack of value for the ERG work at the top of the house. According to a Five-to-Nine article published in 2019, the average ERG gets about $72 per individual (2). There is a broad range here since this number can be as low as $1.37 per member and as high as $370 per member. The average number of employees in an organization who are employee resource group members is about seven-point nine percent (3). So, if you work for a company with five thousand employees, you probably have about three-hundred-and-ninety-five people in various ERGs, and your total budget across all your ERGS is slightly over $28,000. Middle leaders who directly benefit from this work often express appreciation, but they also say their hands are tied when it comes to securing more budget or support. Why? Often, they say they need to get more buy-in from the top. In other words, while these middle-level leaders, like the CHRO and Head of Talent, know the value of the work led by ERG leaders, the CEO seems to be oblivious to all this invisible work going on behind the scenes that hold their organization's workforce and culture together.

On top of these challenges, we pile all the added demands on ERGs in this new post-pandemic and social unrest era of constant disruption. And that's where we are today. So, what can ERG leaders do to address these old lingering challenges that predate 2020, plus all the new ones? In addition to becoming more adept at scanning the future horizon for what's coming, the following is a list of ten other areas where ERG leaders need to develop new approaches.

1. ERG leaders need to learn how to do less to achieve more.
2. ERG leaders need to learn how to get the CEO's attention.
3. ERG leaders need to learn to lead an ERG in this new, more complex workplace.
4. ERG leaders need to learn to help the organization design equity into their systems instead of piling more patchwork on their ERGs plates.
5. ERG leaders need to enhance their skills without losing more valuable personal time.
6. ERG leaders need to learn how to leverage more of the new tools and resources appearing on the scene.
7. ERG leaders need to learn how to expand their footprint across the workforce.
8. ERG leaders need to speed up the lines of communication across and up and down the organization.
9. ERG leaders need to learn how to impact the emerging world of AI proactively.
10. ERG leaders need to learn how to get all their members fully engaged and spread the responsibility across a wider net instead of having it all sit on their shoulders.

In the remainder of this chapter, we will look at ten tips you can use to get your ERGs up to speed in meeting these challenges, old and new, in record time.

The Ten Tips for ERG Leaders Facing the New Frontier

Tip 1 – Stop Being a Multi-Tasker and Start Being a Multi-Achiever

Multitasking refers to the idea of you splitting your attention across more than one task or activity at the same time, such as speaking on the phone while driving a car. Many people who practice multitasking believe they are being more productive. Unfortunately, what they may be achieving is raising their mistake and stress levels.

The first published use of the word "multitask" appears to have been in an IBM paper describing the capabilities of the IBM System/360 back in 1965. Around that same time, the term started being applied to human activities. Since then, many researchers have explored the nature and limits of human multitasking. Their findings tend to support what we intuitively know to be true.

We humans can and often do perform more than one task at a time. For example, most of us can walk and chew gum. But neither of these tasks require a significant amount of conscious attention. For the most part, they are driven by our unconscious programs that handle several automatic routines and functions. On the other hand, our overall performance degrades when we attempt to do more than one thing that requires our conscious attention. This, according to experts, is due to the time we waste switching our conscious attention between each task. Why? Because we literally cannot pay equal conscious attention to two things simultaneously. When we push ourselves splitting our attention this way, we make wasteful errors due to insufficient attention and feeling stressed out.

So, what can an ERG leader who faces demands to meet multiple needs from their regular job plus an additional four goals through their ERG demands do? The answer is to become a multi-achiever. So, what is a multi-achiever, and how does it differ from a multi tasker. The best way to explain is through a few examples.

The first one is a story I came across when interviewing Lynn Yapp, Managing Director of Activ8 Network, and the author of "The Altruistic Capitalist." The conversation took place while taping a future episode of the ERG PowerTalk podcast. Part of Yap's work and passion involves promoting the participation of women in innovation, technology, and entrepreneurship. One of her past projects involved working with a women's group at Pearson Education. Pearson is a British-owned education publishing and assessment service to schools, corporations, and students directly. They own several educational media brands, including Addison–Wesley, Peachpit, Prentice-Hall, eCollege, Longman, and Scott Foresman. The group Yap was working with had four goals. One was to have a business impact. The second was to have a community impact.

The third was to build the connection between women in different silos across Pearson. And the fourth was to develop their members' leadership skills. A multitasking approach here would have meant pursuing at least four projects, one for each goal, and trying to run all four simultaneously. That's not what they did. Instead, they focused on one project that satisfied all four objectives. Here's how they did it.

One of Pearson's brands wanted to develop a new product whose target market was students going to college. The women's group partnered with the new product team. They launched a mentorship and coaching program with college-bound girls in a local school to gain valuable insights on how to bring the product to market while shaping the target market's opinions. The group participants in this effort received training in coaching and mentoring. They met, connected, and worked with the students. The information and relationships they built ultimately helped the company launch its new product successfully.

Here are just four of the goals met by this single project:

- **Membership Impact**. It developed the skills of the women participants as leaders through training in coaching, mentoring, and hands-on experience.
- **Community Impact.** It built community and market goodwill for Pearson.
- **Business Impact.** It provided the information needed for a new product launch as well as an open the door to a relationship with this new market
- **More Business Impact.** It enabled women from various parts of Pearson to connect in a common cause and develop internal relationships across silos.

A second example comes from my days working for Siemens. One of the Siemens ERGs was a Latinx group seeking to achieve four goals. One, have a measurable impact on the business. Two, develop a strong network in the external Latinx community near the corporate office. Three, develop the career visibility of the Latinx members of the ERG. And four bring insightful and exciting speakers to their members. To accomplish all of these in one effort, they partnered with a sales team looking for opportunities to sell Siemens services to cities and municipalities.

Essentially, this sales team worked with cities and municipalities to convert abandoned industrial plots of land, called brownfield zones, and turn them back into productive use. (They leased equipment, provided financing, and worked with the local government to ensure expected tax revenues more than covered the loans). With the partnership in place, the ERGs went to an event where they connected with local Latinx leaders. One happened to be the mayor of a nearby town with many brownfield areas. The ERG leaders provided the appropriate introductions, which led to a win-win for the business and the community. Community leaders were more than happy to come and speak at events held by the ERG.

So, let's tally up how this effort met the ERGs four goals:

- □ **Measurable Business Impact**. This effort resulted in a long-term and lucrative business relationship between the company and a major city.
- □ **Strong External Community Network.** The network's value to the community enabled them to connect with its highest levels of government.
- □ **Develop Career Visibility for the Members and Leaders.** The outcome of this project put all the members involved and the ERG leader on the company CEO's radar.
- □ **Secure Insightful External Speakers from the Community Leadership.** Members of the external community's government leadership were more than happy to come and speak at this ERGs event.

And for good measure, here is the third example I picked up in an interview with the leader of a Veterans effort in a non-profit hospital. Aaron Harper is a marine I interviewed for an ERG PowerTalk episode back in 2019. Harper works for Atrium Health as an HR Strategic Business Partner. Notice I say that Harper is a marine, not a former marine. That's because when you talk to Harper, you get the sense that there will never be anything former about his time as a marine. He noted that he was a fifth-generation marine in his family with a wife who was a National Guard Colonel and Helicopter Pilot.

When I spoke to Harper, he was manager of military and veteran's affairs. So more of a formal practice leader than an ERG effort leader, but I believe ERG leaders can follow his example. Harper's goals included developing senior-level stakeholder support and community support based on value to these stakeholders. He recognized that for his organization, the care of patients was the primary goal. One of his key efforts involved working with a senior medical leader to create a partnership between Atrium's Carolina Medical Center and Fort Bragg. In essence, this brought doctors, nurses, emergency medical technicians, paramedics, etc., from the military to work alongside their counterparts in a civilian trauma center. "It's a great symbiotic relationship that we have with them," says Harper. This military-medical personnel participating in this joint effort, acquire the tools and experience to address the medical issues of the civilian populations they encounter during their deployment overseas. On the flip side, the local trauma center's medical personnel gains valuable experience in treating the kinds of things their military counterparts have more experience treating on the battlefield. These include injuries, like blunt force trauma, bullet injuries, and severe cuts.

Now, let's pause and think about all the goals met by this one effort in a non-profit setting:

- □ **Impact on the Non-Profits Mission**. This effort made it possible to provide a higher quality of service to the non-profit community.
- □ **Impact on the Non-Profit Community Relationship.** This effort made the non-profit a top provider of services to their community and, as such, a valued member.
- □ **Increased Appreciation for the Value of Military Experience.** Working together grew the mutual respect and connection between this civilian operation and its military counterpart. This increases the likelihood that some military personnel would want to work at this hospital upon concluding their military service. The hospital, in turn, would be more than happy to welcome them on board.

- **Senior-Level Support for the Effort.** This effort produced results that made the hospital a top decile provider, employer, and community member. Those are the kinds of results that get the support of a non-profit healthcare leader.

And those are just a few examples of the power of multi-achievement efforts.

So, what are the key things you need to look for in finding opportunities for multi-achievements?

Step 1- First, identify the specific goals you would like to meet to address current challenges. (Impact mapping as described in Chapter 5 of SuperCharge Your ERGs can help you do this).

Step 2- Next, look for opportunities to partner with the business to fulfill your goals through one effort. According to Yap, this is where the best options for meeting multiple objectives can be found. I agree. Business projects generally offer an opportunity to hit many goals while contributing measurable value to the overall organization. In a non-profit organization, business goals are closely tied with the non-profits mission or another way of saying it would be its reason for existence.

Step 3–Finally, execute your one or two multi-achievement projects and track your results.

Multitasking will not cut it in today's super-fast, super busy, ever-changing world. I invite you to step up your results with less busy work and effort by mastering the art of multi-achieving. Be picky when looking for projects and partners. Instead of signing up to support a small recruiting project here and a little talent development project over there, plus an external community project in some other area, look for one significant effort. More than likely, you won't find projects like that anywhere other than at the heart of your business.

Tip 2 – How to Get and Keep VITOs Scarce Attention

When I talk about VITO here, I'm not referring to a person with that name. I'm talking about the Very Important Top Officer in your organization. That in many organizations is a CEO, a President, or a Senior Managing Partner. The term VITO referring to the Very Important Top Officer was created in 1995 by Tony Parinello, a former salesman who wrote a series of books about selling to VITO. Parinello's key point was simple. If you want to do rapid business without spinning your wheels too much, you need to get VITO's attention and buy-in. The same is true for DEI and ERG leaders who want to succeed in today's fast-paced world.

In today's world, you need to act quickly to avoid obstacles and seize opportunities. You cannot succeed if your communications and request are doomed to join your senior leader's stack of "I'll get to it when I have time" pile. You will simply not be able to pounce on the most significant opportunities or have the biggest impact. You'll also have difficulty securing the type of funding often needed to achieve significant goals. You need to capture and engage the attention and support of that Very Important Top Officer in your company to do that. So, what's the obstacle between you and VITO, and how do you get past it?

"The most precious thing that a CEO has to spend is our time. It's not our money. It's our time. It is the thing we don't have ever enough of and what we have to prioritize constantly." That's a quote from Catherine Jacobson, President, and CEO of Froedtert Health. It's a statement that is probably truer today than ever before in a world of constant disruption. Jacobson explains that if you have ERGs engaged in things that "are a nice thing to do," like employee engagement efforts, the most you can expect to receive from a CEO is a small amount of attention. Not because the CEO doesn't care about these things. Many of them do. It's just that they are constantly pressed for time in areas where they need to deliver personally. When it comes to these "nice to do" things, the CEO will look to someone else like a person in HR to take care of you. Maybe the CEO can carve out a little personal time for these nice-to-do things once a year. And that's about it. On the other hand, if your ERG is working on things directly linked to the CEO's success, you're going to get a lot more personal time, focus, and attention from your CEO.

So, what are the vital things that will get you to the top of the CEO's attention list, and where can you learn more about these opportunities? Here are three things to consider:

Step 1–Find the tip-of-the-spear in your business and align yourself to support it. If you are in a for-profit business, you will likely find this opportunity in one of your revenue-driving business units. There are many examples of ERGs that have helped their organizations score millions and billions of dollars in new business. Reach out to front-line business units and explore the opportunities to partner. If, on the other hand, you are in a non-profit, your opportunity to get on the CEO's radar will be in one of the units that most directly enables your company to deliver on its mission. For example, Froedtert's critical mission is to serve its patients as a healthcare organization. By helping the organization create Public Safety Announcement designed to overcome vaccine hesitancy in their communities, Froedtert's ERGs provided value in an area that was very important to their CEO.

Step 2–As a group leader, think like VITO for your group. Value your time and your group's time. Don't squander it on too many "nice to do things." Now, don't get me wrong. I'm not saying you don't do any "nice to do" things. Just don't make that the lion's share of your efforts. Give it what Jacobson calls "a nice thing to do level of attention."

Step 3–Invest your time in projects, not programs. A project is a discrete set of activities with a beginning, a middle, and an ending. A program is an ongoing delivery of services. As the leader of a group of volunteers who have full-time jobs, you don't want to weigh yourself or others down with taking on the role of another full-time job. Suppose your organization regularly needs some service or product into the foreseeable future. In that case, it probably should be somebody's full-time job and not an activity performed by a group of volunteers. Avoid letting yourself or your group get pulled into those situations. They seldom involve doing anything that rises to the level of your very important top officer's attention, but they do put a drag on your time.

The key message here is to get VITOs attention, focus on things that matter to VITO. And start thinking like a VITO. Pick and choose wisely how you will invest your time and the time and energy of your group members.

Tip 3 – Expand Your Membership by Leading a Four-Dimensional ERG

As I am writing this chapter, there are many articles on remote work and leading hybrid teams. Hybrid teams are defined as a group of employees composed of people who work from their company's workplace and remotely. Naturally, as the company's workforce management strategy moves from single campus-centric to hybrid, ERG leaders will be encouraged to do the same with how they lead their ERGs.

But I don't think a hybrid strategy is enough. Based on my research, a better strategy is a multidimensional one. This approach addresses the four dimensions of work we covered earlier. These, again, are the same place at the same time, the same place at different times, different place at the same time, and different place at different times. We can also refer to these as traditional in-campus work, shift work, online synchronous meetings, and online asynchronous work.

Based on my research on our workplace's direction, getting yourself and your group acclimated to this multidimensional approach will bring you huge current and future benefits. These include the following:

- First, you will immediately maximize the number of people your group can attract and engage. As we learned earlier, Dollar General's ERGs experienced a dramatic expansion of their reach and engagement across the company's hundred-thousand-plus distributed workforce by just reaching out to the remote work dimension. Imagine the impact of embracing all dimensions?
- Second, you and your group members will gain valuable experience to prepare you to operate and thrive in the future workplace. As noted earlier, we're not sure that even thirty percent of the workforce will still be in the same place at the same time category. Broadening your reach across all dimensions of the workplace ensures your groups will continue to grow and thrive regardless of which dimensions of the workplace grow, shrink, or stagnate.
- And finally, here's the third benefit. Your group will take the lead in providing cross-dimensional cultural glue. A glue that

firmly holds together members of a workforce distributed across the many dimensions of the workplace.

So how can you build, engage, and lead a multidimensional group that draws, engages, and supports members across all the dimensions of the modern and future workplace? Here's a simple example for you to consider. The approach covers what you do before, during, and after an event to engage the maximum number of people across every workplace dimension. It's a composite of the many practices I've seen successfully used by other ERG groups over a decade of interviews. And it uses tools that already exist and are available in most organizations and easy-to-follow tips.

So, let's set the stage for our example. Say you have a guest speaker on the topic of gender equity. The speaker will be at one of your California workplace offices between 9 am, and 10:30 am PST. You want to capture and engage the biggest audience for this speaker from across all your workplace dimensions. Here's what you can do.

Step 1 – In addition to the typical event committee members that include someone who announces the event and records the RSVPs of people coming in person, also identify a team of three additional event coordinators. These include the following roles. One, someone who will introduce the speaker and coordinate the activities in the room where people are meeting with the speaker in person. Two, someone who will set up and coordinate the online environment where remote guests will be joining the event. And three, someone who will be in the online environment recording the meeting on their computer to later stream it to shift and asynchronous working team members.

Step 2 – When you announce your event, make sure you convey three ways to participate. One, by attending in person at the designated time in the designated place. Two, by logging into the virtual platform. Three, by visiting the site where the meeting video will be hosted and joining a moderated discussion with comments and questions.

Step 3 – Make sure the person handling the group meeting announcement records the names of interested participants and how they will participate. So, let's say, continuing with our example, you determine that thirty people will be in the meeting room in California between 9 am and 10:30 am PST. Another seventy tell you they will be on the remote platform simultaneously. And another fifty say they will be participating at different times from different places. That's a total potential audience of one-hundred-and-fifty people.

Step 4 – On the day of the meeting, your three event coordinators begin fifteen minutes early to enable in-person and hybrid attendees to network and settle in before your guest speaker is brought on. Your coordinator at the campus welcomes and hosts people as they arrive. Meanwhile, your online coordinator does the same with people as they log into the platform. Your coordinator for the asynchronous streaming is also signed into the online platform as a co-host. They use this time to prepare to begin recording once the formal meeting kicks off.

Step 5 – The online meeting coordinator and participants can engage in silent text chats when the meeting kicks off. These can focus on various questions or comments about what the speaker is saying. (This is an effective way to engage and maintain online participant attention and engagement). During the question-and-answer session with the speaker, the online coordinator can bring online questions to the speaker's attention in one of two ways. One, by asking the question on behalf of the online guest. Or two, if the online guests are connected to the in-room sound system, by raising their hand and securing the floor for one of their online guests to pose their question directly to the speaker.

Step 6 – After the meeting is concluded, the asynchronous guest coordinator will post the meeting video to a secure site where only the invited can view and comment on the video. Along with posting the video and a description of the topic, this coordinator will pose questions or comments designed to stir discussion threads. Next, they will invite the people on their list of participants who wanted to engage with the topic asynchronously.

Taking these six simple steps can immediately increase your reach and expand the value and impact of your ERG across your entire workforce.

Tip 4 – Invest Time in Helping Build Equity

Equity, as one of my ERG PowerTalk podcast guests, author Minal Bopaiah often points out, is a topic that is often misunderstood and seldom given the attention of its two companions in the DEI acronym. Diversity is about the mix of people in an organization. Inclusion is about inviting, encouraging, and supporting full participation in resources, activities, and recognition. Equity, however, is about designing systems, practices, and policies that enable your team members to participate to the best of their abilities.

Building equity is of the utmost importance as we move into the future. If an organization does not build on equity, most of its DEI and ERG gains can vanish just as quickly as they appeared. This is the kind of staled progress we've seen for the past decades where organizations rise and fall in their DEI results with an almost predictable rhythm. On the other hand, when your organization builds on equity, you create more robust and longer-lasting solutions. When you invest in producing more equitable systems and policies, you are transforming the organization at its very core into a place that can embrace and leverage more diversity inclusively. The fact is that most organizations have significant challenges and opportunities that can only be addressed through measures that build equity. Here's a quick personal story that brings that point home.

Many years ago, before I entered the DEI space, I was the head of a 300 employee IT outsourcing organization. In the outsourcing world, signing a letter of intent for a new outsourcing deal is a cause for celebration. Still, revenue will not flow into the firm until a new program management team delivers services. One critical element needed is a new Program Executive. In short, if you cannot find or promote someone to take on the role of Program Executive over the new account management team, you cannot begin to deliver on the contract, and there is no earned revenue.

So, with that background, you can understand my frustration when we could not find enough qualified Program Executives to quickly take on all the new clients our sales team was signing on. Another fact that did not escape my notice is that all our Program Executives were males. Despite the growing number of females joining the company, only men made it to the top. I set out to find out why this was the case. It was in my business interest to make sure that females had equal opportunities to reach the top.

It was good for the female workforce and the company. I discovered a classic case of a historical inequity blocking equal opportunity.

You see, about 90 percent of the men who joined the firm took technical roles, either programming software or assembling and fixing computer hardware. On the other hand, 90 percent of the women who joined the company took logistics, help desk, and different administrative roles. To become a Service Manager who was on the path to becoming a Program Executive, an employee needed to understand technical and administrative processes and get the "big picture." The company had an excellent development program to teach technical people about this administrative side of the business. However, the company did not have an equivalent program to teach someone who came through the administrative side about the technical end of the business. That was why many men had a path to the top, and many women had a short ladder that did not.

Hiring more women under this structure would just pile and trap more women at the bottom. So, increasing diversity efforts would not solve this challenge. More inclusion wouldn't solve this problem either. Even if more women were brought into the program designed for the technical men, it would not have provided what they needed. I needed more Program Manager candidates, and I was convinced that we could find and develop them from among the bright professional women in the company with the right approach. I just needed to give them an equal opportunity to succeed. Although we didn't use the term back then, we needed an equity solution. We needed to build another path that supported the development of these team members in the administrative part of the company.

After meeting with my direct reports, we came up with an initial solution. We proposed a shadowing program for people who joined through the administrative path that would expose them to work done on the technical side of the equation. The result was an immediate increase in the number of females becoming Service Managers, followed by more female Program Executives. Many years later, many of those females continued to rise to even higher levels within the company.

By the way, this equity program did not tip the balance in favor of the team members who came through the administrative track. It simply gave them the same opportunity as the predominantly male team members who came in via the technical path. In short, it leveled up another group and gave them the chance to reach for the top. There can be no argument here supporting claims of disadvantaging one group to help another.

So, what are some of the steps you and your groups can take to build equity for your community and members?

Step 1 – Start paying more attention to policies and system designs. Say you lead a women's ERG, and you want to increase the number of successful women in sales. Start by taking note of all the systemic components that support sales success. In your list, you might notice that being reimbursed for expenses related to client meetings is one of those factors. On closer inspection, you might see that all expenses generally incurred by men, like drinks with prospects and clients, are covered. Meanwhile, some of the expenses a female salesperson might incur, like a babysitter for her toddler, are not covered. That gives the male salesperson an advantage over the female due to lack of proper support.

Step 2 – Another way to uncover equities in support is to look for how gaps in institutional support are being filled by extraordinary means by people held up as examples of success. So, using the same women's ERG example, let's say during a Women's History Month celebration, you have a successful female executive speaker. Instead of talking about her success, ask your speaker to discuss the extraordinary things that support her success. She may have a stay-at-home-husband who cares for their children. Or she may be the beneficiary of having a wealthy family. Next, compare this with what the successful men need to do to supplement the support offered by the company toward their success. If the women need to fill more gaps, then the men, ask "why is that the case? What is the company failing to offer to support their female talent equally, and how can they address that?"

Step 3 – Present your findings and recommendations to your DEI team.

Any ERG can run through these same steps for any community group. By searching and presenting your findings on opportunities to build equity for your communities, you will be contributing to your company's long and short-term success as a place that attracts and leverages the best talent across all dimensions of diversity. This is always a better approach than having your ERG take on more "patch-the-bad-process" work.

Tip 5 – Claim Your Space in the Fifth Dimension

As good as online meeting platforms are, they have some common shortcomings. For one thing, they make it harder to pick up and discern nonverbal clues that enrich communication during in-person meetings. Another is they don't offer much of an opportunity for people to connect and chat randomly and organically in a way that opens new lines of communication. Finally, online platforms require that all participants schedule and plan a specific time to join for a particular purpose. That limits them to use by only members of the workforce working from different places at the same time. Those are areas where the metaverse platform can fill in significant disconnection gaps for the workforce members in any of the current four dimensions of the modern workplace. For those of you that are "geeky" science fiction fans like me, the metaverse probably sounds like a cross-dimensional connection bridge between the other four dimensions of the workplace. That is exactly what it can be. Think of the metaverse as a space wormhole that connects many parts of the modern workplace.

Also, think about all the things you can do in this metaverse. You can set up a meeting conference space for you and your team members. You can attend scheduled meetings in your team's conference room where you and your colleagues can fully interact via your avatars. If you're facilitating a meeting and someone puts their hand up to get your attention, you will see their hand. You and your team can also start work on a project and leave it there, so that shift workers in the same and other buildings can come around later and add their contributions.

You can also have your parallel universe metaverse office. This can be a replica of your physical home or business office in the metaverse. A notice can alert you when someone is knocking on your metaverses virtual door. You can choose to let them enter and join them in the room or let them know when you'll be available. If you're not around, your visitor can leave you a note saying they dropped by and would like to see you briefly.

Or perhaps, you may choose to have an open-door metaverse policy. In this case, you enter your metaverse office in the morning and work at your desk. Co-workers from any of the other four dimensions can simply pop in to visit you. Or you can step out of your metaverse office and visit a colleague in another virtual office.

Likewise, you can set up an ERG metaverse meeting room. Here your ERG members can get together for scheduled meetings. Or they can pop in from different places at different times to check out work performed by others towards the group's goals. In this space, they can pick up valuable assets like a meeting recording or make and leave their contributions for other group members.

Now, all of this may be making your head spin. That's because it's hard to grasp ideas around experiences you've never had. For example, you can't fully convey the feeling of dancing through words to someone who does not dance. The same is true with the feeling of swimming or playing any number of sports. Many things like these and learning to converse in a new language can only be learned through immersion. That's why I recommend you start getting familiar with this fifth dimension of the workplace right now. How? Here are a few steps you can take:

Step 1 – Enter the metaverse. Start by dipping a toe in the water. For a few hundred dollars, you and one or two of your ERG leadership team members can get VR headsets and gloves. Next, you can set up an account for yourself in one of the gaming platforms like Sandbox, Roblox, Minecraft, Second Life, etc. Playing within the metaverse is one of the ways to increase your familiarity with this new space.

Step 2 – Start thinking of ways to do productive work relative to your ERG goals within the metaverse. "Most metaverse platforms, such as Roblox and Minecraft, are designed primarily for fun, not work. But many of the builders of these virtual spaces have organically realized their potential for meeting or coworking," according to a recent article published in Digiday (Lee, 2021). Think about how you would run a meeting or summit there. Consider how people working in all the other physical dimensions of work might engage in this metaverse program? Perhaps it could be a twenty-four-hour event, with people popping in and out as guests and a string of hosts coordinating different segments—a sort of ERG marathon event.

Step 3 – Don't limit yourself to doing just the things you do in the physical world in the metaverse. Release your creativity once you get comfortable in this new, unfettered space. Ask yourself, what can our group do here that is unique and different from what is possible in the physical world? How can we engage and drive inclusion and equity here?

Based on my research, the metaverse is about to get bigger. It will be a place where new signals of the coming future first appear. So, don't wait to be the last to experience it. Jump in early and start thinking about how you and your ERG can drive value from this new and exciting emerging dimension of the workplace.

Tip 6 – Create Sub-Groups for Your Non-Employee Colleagues

Many organizations want to avoid doing any DEI or ERG-related activities that include independent contractors or temporary workers, fearing they might cross the line in treating a contractor or temp as an employee. That's because contractors and temps do not enjoy health and other employee benefits, which could be deemed due to them if they could be proven to be employees. As a result, many ERGs do not include them in their community events or leadership roles.

You may think dealing with these issues is a new and unsolved challenge. But that is not the case. For an example of how you and your ERG can address this challenge, check out what some crowd-sourcing companies are doing. Crowd-sourcing companies are organizations with a small kernel of core employees who farm out the bulk of their productive work to people anywhere in the country or worldwide. There are all kinds of crowdsourcing companies across almost every single industry. These include artificial intelligence development, language training services, hospitality, home maintenance, ground travel service, fashion design, idea development consulting, accounting services, financial services, computer development and administration, and many more. Most of these companies have already cracked the code when it comes to supporting a growing base of non-employees.

A look at Topcoder provides an example of how these companies work. Topcoder is a crowdsourcing company that delivers its computer development and administration services to its clients through an open global community of designers, developers, data scientists, and programmers [(5)]. The company was started in 2001 by a fellow named Jack Hughes. By 2009, Topcoder had sixteen project managers servicing thirty-five clients. But the actual work for these clients was not performed by the employees. It was performed by several of one-hundred-and-seventy contractors registered to work with Topcoder. In 2013, Topcoder merged with Appirio in a buyout, and both companies continued to operate under the Topcoder brand. At that time of that transaction, Topcoder had grown their client base, and their independent contract worker pool swelled to five hundred thousand people. Wipro bought Topcoder along with Appirio in 2016 for $500 million. The most current financials tell us that in 2020, Topcoder earned $20 million in revenue with only one hundred and four employees and an independent contractor pool of 1.5 million [(6)]. How does Topcoder maintain and build a workforce of independent contractors that keeps growing and gives them an almost unlimited supply of project talent, with such a low percentage of employees?

The secret to Topcoder's success in building this pool of non-employee independent contractors is how they develop and maintain an external community. It's a community with competitions, prizes, and events like what some professional associations provide. Topcoder participates in the community as its principal sponsor. But the community is to a great degree self-governed by volunteer advisors from within the community. The result is a growing pool of talent that Topcoder can tap into that is maintained at enough arm's length that none of its members can be mistaken for employees. Okay, so how can we use this proven template to begin to address the challenge of expanding your ERG and DEI tent over non-employees without raising red flags?

How about this for a novel idea? Have your ERG start an external association for your contractors and temps. Call it your External Association Group (EAG). Let's look at how this might work with a Women's ERG. The women's ERG sponsors a group for female professionals who are temps and independent contractors that perform work in their industry. The ERG provides speakers and discussions that center on the needs of female professions in the company's industry. They can also do recognition ceremonies for temps and contractors who did projects for their company. Membership can be open to women who are temps or contractors who have worked for the company in the past or are presently working for the company and those considering working for the company in the future. We can go on, but I'm sure you get the idea.

This can have enormous benefits for your DEI, ERG, and business. Here are just three of those benefits. One, your company gets to bring in the unheard voices and diverse perspectives of what is soon likely to be half the workforce. Two, your company gets to build a continuous connection around a growing pool of flexible talent. Three, you get to nurture and support a more significant portion of your community beyond the employee label without crossing the line.

Here are some steps you can take to get going:

Step 1 – Get the numbers. Find out how many temps and independent contractors work in your company. Next, determine how many of them fall into the demographic your ERG represents (E.g., Women or vets). Your office of DEI can probably get this from HR.

Step 2 – Run this idea by legal to make sure you consider applicable State laws and industry practices.

Step 3 – Assuming you have a green light, talk to a few temps and independent contractors that align with your community demographics and gauge their interest in what you are offering. Let their input shape it.

Step 4 – Ask one of the members of this new community who they would consider as a leader for this external group. Support, coach, and advise, but let them pick their leadership. Also, designate an ERG liaison to act as the communication link between you and this external group.

Step 5 – When they launch, attend, and support the event as agreed.

By following these simple steps, you can extend your DEI and ERG tent to include this growing workforce segment while maintaining compliance with your local laws regarding non-employees.

Tip 7 – Become a Community Pollster

In 1824, in a presidential race between John Quincy Adams and Andrew Jackson, the Harrisburg Pennsylvanian, a local newspaper in Pennsylvania's capital, surveyed Wilmington, Delaware. It asked voters their opinions on the presidential election due that November. The newspaper reported that 70% of respondents intended to vote for Andrew Jackson. Jackson went on to win a narrow popular vote victory, but his opponent John Quincy Adams was elected president by the House of Representatives. That event was the first time an opinion poll was ever conducted [(7)].

In the past, rulers who the people did not elect showed little interest in knowing the opinions and perspectives of the public. That all changed after the French and American revolutions. As gaining leadership became more dependent on "the will of the people," rulers and leaders began to express more interest in their citizens' thinking. The practice of polling was a natural outcome of that need.

Corporate leaders, of course, are not elected by their workforce. But their workforce members are not indentured servants. Their workforce can vote with their feet to stay and support the company mission or invest their talents somewhere else. So, smart corporate leaders that are interested in attracting and engaging the best talent also have a good reason to be interested in the opinions and perspectives of their workforce. And these workforce perspectives also often yield valuable insights into how various segments of the company's total available market see the world. This enables leadership to shape their offerings to serve the needs and wants of a larger market. As Froedtert CEO Catherine Jacobson put it, leaders are literally "flying blind" without these diverse perspectives. That's why I recommend that you become your community's opinion pollster.

By collecting your community's perspectives, you can drive several important outcomes. Here are four ways you can leverage your community polls to drive value. One, it helps you select the most value-driving programs for your membership. Two, it enables you to provide valuable information to your business leaders about engaging the workforce segment represented by your community. Three, it allows you to convey the collective needs of your community to the leaders who are in a position to address those needs and concerns. Four, it provides leadership with valuable insight into the needs and perspectives of clients and potential clients who are part of the community.

So here are seven simple steps you can follow to become your community's pollster:

Step 1 – Establish a clear statement of what you would like to know. For example, the purpose of your survey might be "to learn what our community thinks about the new corporate learning system?" Or "to get the communities perspectives and feelings about going back to the office." It should not be something vague like "to find out what the community wants." Unfocused opinion polls result in responses all over the map and are often useless. If you have multiple topics you would like to explore, use separate polls.

Step 2 – Ask questions that your responder can intelligently answer. So, for example, say you head up a Women's ERG. Don't ask, "do you think most women want to return to the office?" How the heck is the respondent supposed to know what "most women" think? A good question would be, "do you want to go back to the office?" Now you're asking the respondent a question they can answer with available information and insights they possess. A better version of that question for a more granular response might be, "on a scale of 0 for I don't want to return to the office to 5 for I want to go back right away, how would you gauge your desire to go back to the office?" The point here is to ask questions that the respondent can intelligently answer. As a rule, questions that ask the respondent about their feelings and knowledge about their perspectives and feelings are good. Questions that ask the respondent to mind-read the moods and opinions of a group are less valuable.

Step 3 – Collect the responses to your survey and look for patterns. If a large percentage of people in our Women's ERG example say they don't want to go back to the office, that's an important finding.

Step 4 – As you collect significant findings, build additional questions to explore why people feel or perceive things the way they do. So again, continuing with our Women's ERG example, if a large percent say they don't want to return to the office, follow-up questions might be, "why do you think this is the case? What's behind this large consensus?"

Step 5 – Schedule a time to meet with a large sample of the survey participants and conduct a mini-focus group. In this meeting, you can open by sharing the survey's findings and posing your follow-up questions to the participants. Make sure you collect responses and take notes without the names of the respondents. (You want to share the findings while maintaining the confidence and trust of the group to encourage openness).

Step 6 – Combine the survey and focus group findings into a single summary that highlights the information about group perspectives gleaned from the responses and the anecdotal stories that explain what conditions and beliefs may support the perceptions uncovered by the study. In that report, you can also share any recommendations you have.

Step 7 – Use your report to determine programs and efforts the group might undertake. Also, share your findings with the office of DEI so that they can compile them with other group findings and present senior management with a better picture of the perceptions of the diverse workforce communities and suggestions.

As the workforce becomes more diverse, complex, and distributed, this type of community poll service will become increasingly valuable to you as a community leader. It will also become more valuable to your business leaders seeking to compete for business and talent amid this disruption and complexity.

Tip 8 – Integrate Learning into Your Routine

In a world of constant disruption, old knowledge is always becoming obsolete. In fact, according to some commentators, we should apply a form of Gordon Moore's Law to determine the speed of our knowledge decay. According to Moore's Law, the number of transistors on a microchip doubles every eighteen to twenty-four months. This results in doubling computer power and new devices and applications every two years. Just think of all the new tools and potential for commerce and connection between people that have become significant in the last two decades. We've seen the rise of more powerful computing, storage, social media, cloud computing, and artificial intelligence. These have radically changed our day-to-day and business lives. Companies like Uber and Airbnb became possible and disrupted big established industries. These technologies also change how companies hire, how they promote, and how people connect and work together, which impacts many areas that affect you and your ERGs. As these new devices, tools, and applications arrive, they change our world. With these changes, our old practices, knowledge, strategies, and experiences become obsolete.

So, the bottom line is simple here. If you want to stay ahead of the disruption curve and continue growing your career and driving your ERG efforts to succeed in a rapidly changing world, you need to keep learning. One author of a 2017 article in Quartz at Work boldly claimed in his title that "if you're not spending 5 hours per week learning, you're being irresponsible [(8)]." He points out in that article how successful people in all walks of life, like President Obama, Warren Buffett, and Bill Gates, all live by some version of this rule. But how can someone who already has a full-time day job, plus the leadership of an ERG, and hopefully some semblance of a personal life, ever hope to squeeze in five or more hours per week of learning? The answer is simple. Integrate your learning into other activities.

Here's an example of how to do it. Every year, I research 30 to 35 books and scan various topics for my books, articles, speeches, and workshops. It takes me only five hours a week. And it does not interfere with my other activities. What's my secret? I bundle this learning with other activities. For example, I run 5 to 6 days a week for anywhere between 30 to 45 minutes in the morning. This is part of a regular cardio routine. During that time, I also listen to new audiobooks on various topics. Twice a week, I also spend 60-minutes doing resistance training with weights; during this time, I listen to podcasts or timely talks streaming online.

We can all find these opportunities to fit learning into our daily routines with just a bit of effort. Here are some steps you can take to get started.

Step 1- Determine the topics where you need to be knowledgeable. Suppose you are leading a Women's ERG in a technical company. In that case, you may want to keep up with topics like women in tech, your industry, hiring, and promotion practices, as well as skills for elevating your group, and of course, topics relevant to your day job. This first step is crucial because you need to focus your attention to get the best value out of your learning efforts. Ideally, the result of this exercise will be a self-learning curriculum guide—something you can use as a filter to scan the eco-system for topics that are important to you.

Step 2- Find sources for your areas of interest that are easy to bundle with other activities. Audiobooks, podcasts, TedTalks, and a host of other tools can supply you with content. As an ERG leader, you can tap into over 100 thousand dollars of free training and inspiration in our ERG PowerTalk podcast. You can listen to experts like author Howard Ross on social justice and building bridges across groups, Minal Bopaiah on designing equity, and a host of other thought leaders on many other timely topics. To access ERG PowerTalk on your favorite podcast delivery platform, simply follow this link- https://linktr.ee/Joesan58

Step 3 – Next, find a task you can bundle with your learning. This is a practical and productive way to multi-task. The key is to combine the right tasks. First, find something you do that does not require a great deal of your conscious attention. For example, for me, it's running and exercising. For others, it might be going for a regular walk. Or perhaps yours is going on a public commute, driving to and from work, preparing meals, cleaning, etc. Simply find one or more regular routines that you do mostly on autopilot and add a learning component to it.

Step 4 – Periodically review your topic priorities and adjust them as new areas of interest arise. At a minimum, look at your target topics at least once a year.

Leveraging today's modern technology, you don't need to set aside a particular block of time just for learning. You can weave it into several of your other daily routines.

Tip 9 – Support the Improvement of AI for Your Community

In 2018, a man named Ibrahim Diallo was surprised when he found that his employee key card would not allow him entry into the Los Angeles skyscraper where his office was based. A security guard let him into the building, and Diallo immediately went to see his manager. She promised to order a new key card for him right away. This, however, was only the beginning of a day Diallo would never forget.

When he got to his cubicle, he noticed that he was logged out of his work system. A colleague he asked for help told Diallo that the word "Inactive" was listed alongside his name in the list of users. As his day continued, things got worse. After lunch, he had to wait for 10-minutes for a co-worker to let him back into his office. When he got back to his desk, HR called and told him that he had been terminated. According to the HR representative, his manager and director knew nothing about this termination, and she promised to sort it all out. After several emails to increasingly senior executives, the mystery was still unsolved. Sometime that afternoon, two people appeared at Diallo's desk and told him that they had received an email to escort him from the building. Later, Diallo learned that he had been fired by an artificial intelligence (AI) system due to a machine error [(9)].What a painful mess up for Diallo and the company.

This story may come as a surprise to many of us. We don't see Arnold Schwarzenegger look-alike robots or Mr. Smith Agents prowling around our offices as we look around. So, we may not notice the ever-growing presence of AI in our workplaces. But, over the last couple of years, unknown to many of you, more and more of your life and decisions have been influenced by the robot wizards hidden behind the curtain of your HR departments. So, unfortunately, the conditions that led to Mr. Diallo's story are not rare or unique. Nor is that the only way that machines mess up. AI is currently used in companies to decide if you get hired, how much you get paid, and if you should be promoted or given specific assignments. And these machines do make mistakes in all these areas. They are sometimes driven by biases they pick up from their programmers or training materials, as noted earlier in this book.

According to Venjara of ADP, to address these issues, "Most companies are now creating and shaping statements of AI ethics and principles." These statements reduce to writing the firms' commitments toward ethical adoption, usage, and management of AI. These essentially serve as a compass that guides the company's ethical and unbiased use of AI. An excellent example of one of these documents can be found on the ADP website [(10)].

In addition, Venjara explains, several companies also have an AI ethics board. These act as a governance group that reviews the adoption and usage of AI within the organization to ensure that AI-powered tools are used in a manner that aligns with the AI ethics and principles presented in their corporate statement.

And yet another tool used by companies when they are rolling out a new AI program or assessing the operation of an in-service tool is the Bias Impact statement. In this document, the organization spells out things, such as:

- □ What they want to accomplish with the AI tool.
- □ Potential adverse impact to specific communities or groups.
- □ What steps do they believe need to be taken to reduce or eliminate the negative impact?

To effectively leverage these tools to ensure better AI outcomes for your company and community, you don't need to be a programmer. You do, however, need to find a way to get your voice heard and included. Here are a few easy steps you can take.

Step 1- Find out if your head of DEI sits on an AI ethics board or has had input into an AI Statement of Ethics and Principles. Also, find out if your head of DEI is providing information into Bias Impact Statements. If they aren't, please encourage them to do so. (More on this and how DEI leaders can do it in the next chapter).

Step 2 – Once your DEI leader is connected to these resources, volunteer to support them in representing your community. Offer to review the AI Statement of Ethics and Principles and to offer helpful questions and comments from your community. You can collect your community's questions and comments during one of your group meetings where you go over the document. You can do the same thing with Bias Impact Statements.

Step 3 – Send your comments and questions to your DEI leader so that she, in turn, can voice these for you with the governing committee.

As more workforce, workplace, and marketplace decisions and processes are handed over to machines, you must ensure your community's voice is heard at those decision-making tables that guide the deployment and usage of these tools.

Tip 10 – Anchor Yourself and Your Group to Your Perfect Future

A vision is one of the most important things you and your group need to stay on course and succeed during turbulent times. Since most people confuse a vision with a mission, let me take a moment to explain the difference and how these two factors complement each other. A vision statement expresses where you see yourself and your group in the future after you've succeeded in accomplishing what you've set out to do. So, a vision statement for the ABC & Company's Women's ERG might be, "A company where women represent half of the leadership team, and equitably designed processes support their equal opportunity to succeed." A vision statement can be longer or shorter than this. The only requirement is that it needs to be a social fiction about what your world, company, country, etc., will look like in the future. My vision statement for the world due to my company and association's work is captured in a five-minute video you can access on YouTube with this link https://youtu.be/NWIVEfK-P2E. In the end, a vision is about that future state.

On the other hand, a mission is about how you plan to get to the state described in the vision. So, staying with my ABC & Company's Women's ERG example, their mission might be to explore and encourage redesigning company practices and policies to create more equal opportunities for women to succeed in the organization. So, in short, while the vision is where we will be, the mission is how we plan to get there.

"Why is it so important to have a vision at a time of continuous disruption," you might ask? Because without a vision, your decisions and actions will likely be short-term based on the winds of change and without any real progress in any direction. Furthermore, since you have not settled on a destination for your efforts with your team members, they will have difficulty responding in a timely and cohesive way to your leadership direction.

So, what can you do to create a group vision? Here are a few easy steps I use in my workshops.

Step 1 – Start by pulling together a small committee of, say, seven to ten people that represent a good cross-section of diverse perspectives within your group. Ask these members to send you one JPG or PNG formatted picture that captures the essence of how they see the organization as a result of their community efforts, in ten years. So, say it's a women's ERG, a female CEO if you don't have one, might be part of your vision. Ask your team members submitting pictures to be bold and give them a set deadline of, say, seven days to respond with their image. Also, ask them to describe how this picture captures where they see themselves and the group when this vision is realized.

Step 2–As people submit pictures and their perspectives, download them, and save them in a folder labeled, our Pictures for our ERG Vision for the future. Then, in that same folder, have a document containing the various descriptions of the future shared by the people who submitted the pictures.

Step 3–Next, use a graphic tool to put all your collected pictures into a collage. I like to use Canva at https://www.canva.com. At the time I write this, the features you need are available free of charge. Once you are in Canva, do the following.

- □ Click on CREATE A DESIGN,
- □ Next, Click on PHOTO COLLAGE
- □ After that, click on ELEMENTS and scroll down to Grids. From here, pick a grid that has enough boxes to hold all your pictures and click on it.
- □ Now click on UPLOADS and upload all the pictures submitted to you. Once you have the pictures in the Canva system, click and drag them into the boxes on your grid frame.

When you are done, you will have a vision board collage that combines all the pictures sent to you. To download and save your vision board collage, do the following:

- □ Click on the downward-pointing arrow in the upper right-hand corner of your CANVA menu.

- It will suggest a PDF download. Change that by clicking on the downward pointing carat and scroll up to select PNG as your file type.
- Now click the DOWNLOAD button and wait for your file.

Step 4–Open your presentation software and bring the PNG file you downloaded with your vision board collage into a blank slide. Below the picture open a text box and write your first draft of the collective vision you see embodied in the collage that captures the sentiment of the comments and the pictures submitted to you. Again, this statement should not be about what you will do or how you will do it. It should simply be a statement that captures your collective future dream of what the world will look like in ten years, for your community in your organization due to your success.

Step 5 – Call a meeting with all the contributors of pictures and perspectives and share your collage and draft summary of a vision. Invite them to comment, modify, and add to it as they see fit. Just remember to make sure that the final product presents a future state as if it were accomplished. Avoid using these phrases:

- We hope to be.
- We will strive.
- Etcetera.

Staying with our women's ERG example, you might have. "We celebrate our first female C-level executive." Or "our benefits and policies provide all women with opportunities to succeed equally to what we offer men." Remember, this is what mission accomplished will look like.

Step 6 – After you've made any edits that come out of this meeting, update your slide, and call a meeting of the entire group. Present them with the small committee's current version and ask the whole group for their feedback. At the conclusion of this meeting, you will have your final collective vision board and vision statement.

Given the multi-dimensional, distributed nature of work, I recommend doing all these steps using online meetings. Also, remember to include representatives from your group that work in all the different workplace dimensions.

Working ON Your ERGs Versus IN Your ERGs

As author Clara Henschke so eloquently puts it, ERGs perform priceless work. As many CDOs I've interviewed over the last few months have said, ERGs have emerged as the clear heroes and heroines of corporate cultures during this time of unrest. I believe they will continue to be an essential and evolving factor in the success of organizations as we face the new frontier.

But to be successful, ERG leaders need to invest some time working ON their groups versus just working IN their groups. This is a phrase I've borrowed from the world of business leadership coaching, where we often differentiate between working ON the business versus IN the business. The phrase was first coined by the author Michael Gerber, who wrote several books on developing businesses. Here's what Gerber referred to when he talked about working ON the business versus IN the business. A leader is working in the business when they are leading or executing the work of the business. So, for example, if you run a bakery and you are making pies or leading your team in pie-making, you are working IN the business.

On the other hand, if you are learning about new techniques to improve the baking process or documenting recipes so that you can hire others to bake your pies in your absence, you are working ON your business. So as an ERG leader, when you are running a member meeting or putting a program together for your members, you are working IN the group's business. However, when you are developing a new skill or creating a new vision for the group to drive them to a new level, you are working ON the group's business. Another way to think of this is that you are working IN the group's business when you are executing the group's plan. However, when working ON the group's business, you are developing the group's capacity to perform at a new level in the future. You are improving the machinery via which the group gets its work done. That's what all these tips are about. They are all about working ON your group business.

I urge ERG leaders to take the time to put these tips to work and to use them to develop their groups' capabilities. I'm confident that the effort you invest will pay back dividends by saving you time and effort and making you more effective in facing current and future challenges.

Bibliography

1. Henschke, Clara. Paying for Priceless Work: A Case for Compensating ERG Leaders. s.l. : Cultivate. https://www.cultivateall.com/blog/paying-erg-leaders.
2. Employee Resource Groups (ERGs): A Key Part of Your Inclusion Strategy. s.l. : Five to Nine, 2019. https://medium.com/@info_37650/employee-resource-groups-ergs-a-key-part-of-your-inclusion-strategy-c6929627cf9d.
3. Employee Resource Group. s.l. : Wikipedia. https://en.wikipedia.org/wiki/Employee_resource_group.
4. Lee, Alexandar. Companies are coworking in the metaverse to stave off Zoom burnout and spark new types of collaboration. s.l. : Digiday, 2021. https://digiday.com/marketing/companies-are-coworking-in-the-metaverse-to-stave-off-zoom-burnout-and-spark-new-types-of-collaboration/.
5. Topcoder. s.l. : Wikipedia. https://en.wikipedia.org/wiki/Topcoder.
6. Topcoder. s.l. : Zoominfo, 2020. https://www.zoominfo.com/c/topcoder-inc/79577206.
7. Rhodes, Campbell. A Brief History of Opinion Polls. s.l. : The Museum of Australian Democracy, 2018. https://www.moadoph.gov.au/blog/a-brief-history-of-opinion-polls/#.
8. Simmons, Michael. If you're not spending 5 hours per week learning, you're being irresponsible. s.l. : Quartz at Work, 2017. https://qz.com/work/1124490/5-hour-rule-if-youre-not-spending-5-hours-per-week-learning-youre-being-irresponsible/.

9. Wakefield, Jane. The man who was fired by a machine. s.l. : BBC, 2018. https://www.bbc.com/news/technology-44561838.

10. Ethics in Artificial Intelligence s.l. :ADP. https://www.adp.ca/-/media/adp/redesign2018/pdf/data-privacy/ai-ethics-statement.pdf

CHAPTER 6

Ten Tips for Chief Diversity Officers

*"Give me six hours to chop down a tree and I will spend the first four sharpening the axe."–**Abraham Lincoln***

Search the Internet high and low, and you won't find an exact date for when it began. Perhaps it was when organizations started to get a better sense of the actual value of increasing and leveraging their diversity. We know that it was after the events of the early 1960s and 1970s that launched the entire diversity training industry. Somewhere amid the growing in-house efforts to address compliance concerns and harness the power of diversity toward the end of the last century, the Chief Diversity Officer role was born.

The chief diversity officer is an executive-level leadership role. Not all companies use the title Chief Diversity Officer. Some refer to it as the VP of Diversity or the Global Head of Diversity. Still, others add from the alphabet soup of terms that keep appearing in our lexicon to create titles like Chief Diversity, Equity, and Inclusion Office. (I'm waiting to hear of the Chief JEDI Officer for Chief Justice, Equity, Diversity, and Inclusion Officer!) According to Wikipedia, whatever we call the role, less than 20 percent of Fortune 500 companies had one in 2005. Over the last fifteen-plus years, that number has grown, with quite a few new executive DEI leadership roles opening during 2020, after the George Floyd murder [(1)].

Like the role of the ERG leader, the role of the diversity chief has evolved over the years. While many CDOs still report into HR, a legacy from the days when their primary responsibility was to create the organization's strategy for recruiting from under-represented communities, today it's a management strategy with a broad reach into all business segments. In some organizations, CDOs now report directly to the CEO. Still, while others continue to report to the HR leader on paper, their responsibilities transcend the HR silo.

In the 2021 CDO PowerCircle Future Foresight Summit, a panel led by Sheryl Battles, CDO Vice President, Global Diversity, Inclusion and Engagement at Pitney Bowes, explored the role of the CDO, post-pandemic, and social unrest. Members of the panel came from several well-known companies in various industries. They included Paul Martin, SVP CDO at SONY Pictures Entertainment, Erica Fletcher, Global Head of Diversity, and Inclusion at Hiscox, Darcy Pierson, CDO at Oshkosh, and Neddy Perez, Global Head of Diversity and Inclusion Center of Excellence for McCormick & Company. The conversation centered on how the work and the demands of the role are evolving. Here's a summary of a few of the key points I got out of this powerhouse discussion:

- DEI leaders need to address an ever-growing array of challenges and opportunities. These include diversity, inclusion, equity, social justice, belonging, and the list continues to grow.
- The scope of the work across the organization is also growing. In addition to being increasingly involved in addressing challenges and opportunities across the entire employee lifecycle, CDOs are now being pulled into challenges with the various dimensions that make up the workplace and marketplace.
- As a result, CDOs need to connect with more stakeholders than ever before.
- The CDO also needs to master more key business topics than ever before.
- CDOs need to continue driving DEI through a culture that is now distributed.
- More CDOs are seeing their role become accountable to shareholders.
- Another challenge facing CDOs is helping business leaders to become more effective in making better decisions in handling these DEI-related opportunities and challenges.

I think these are all spot-on observations. And in my research, I've found that most diversity offices are not staffed or funded to the degree that they can just throw Office of Diversity money and people at these new opportunities and challenges. Instead, they need to strengthen their extended informal team of leaders and supporters. These include Office of Diversity personnel, ERG leaders, ERG members, ERG Executive Sponsors, Liaisons and Partners heading up other significant segments of the organization, etc.

- □ Furthermore, my research findings are that the most powerful things a CDO can do to prepare them to lead in the new frontier are the following:
- □ Ensure that DEI is embedded in the organization's vision.
- □ Provide a structure that links all DEI efforts throughout the organization and speedily coordinates actions.
- □ Provide broader governance for the formal and informal DEI structure to ensure its continued smooth operation.
- □ Provide trusted advice to the CEO and members of the CEO's team.
- □ Help senior leaders find ways to design for increased equity across the workplace and marketplace.
- □ Help guide organizational developments so that they support DEI.
- □ Develop critical supporters and stakeholders of DEI.
- □ Build tomorrow's diverse leadership bench.
- □ Continue to scan the future for opportunities and threats and provide roadmaps for appropriate action.
- □ Continuously develop a more equitable and inclusive version of themselves that appreciates an even broader spectrum of diverse perspectives.

If these sound like challenges that require more working ON the DEI practice instead of working IN the DEI practice, you have been paying close attention. Because that is precisely what is needed. To that end, I invite you to consider the following ten tips.

Building Your DEI Practice for Success Today and In the Future

Tip 1 – Integrate DEI into the Organization's Strategy

We discussed building a vision for resource groups in an earlier tip for ERG leaders. However, when it comes to the overarching vision for DEI, which should be integrated directly within the organization's vision. The same is true for the overall mission of DEI. To succeed, it must be either a natural part of the organization's mission or an extension of that central company mission.

The vision and mission of an organization is a powerful element that permeates the workplace and becomes manifest in the actions of leaders and team members in the workplace. These statements and all clarifying statements attached to them become almost the organizational constitution against which all other policies and rules are measured. Anchoring your DEI vision and mission to the organization's central guiding principles makes DEI a more robust and compelling factor in your company.

Finally, you want to ensure that your DEI strategy is part of the corporate strategy, not a separate strategy. This calls for working closely with the CEO and the CEOs team to ensure that DEI is weaved into all elements of the business strategy (E.g., Business, Strategic Workforce Planning, etc.).

Here are some steps you can follow to do this:

Step 1–Find and read your company's vision and mission statements.

Step 2 – If elements of DEI are not present in these statements, ask yourself how DEI can support and further progress towards the vision and bolster the mission. For example, let's say your vision is to be the number one provider of a delightful vacation experience globally. To that end, your mission is to continue to bring the most powerful level of that experience to people in every corner of the earth. You can probably put the following items on your list of how DEI supports this vision and mission:

- □ We collectively become global citizens that fully understand how to produce "wow" in people of all walks of life because we are them, and we know their values, needs, and perspectives.

- □ We do this by diversifying our leadership and workforce to reflect the world around us, which increases our ability to understand how to produce that powerful experience in people with different values, perspectives, and conditions.
- □ We attract and engage the best talent across all dimensions of diversity by creating the most equitable and inclusive environment.
- □ We expand our total available market by increasing our understanding and reaching into all the communities that make up our market.

I could add more to this list, but I think this is enough to make the point. These statements add a dimension of DEI to the corporate vision and mission.

Step 3 – Present this to your CEO and their immediate team. Ideally, you can aim to have your vision and mission rewritten to include these elements of DEI within them. If that's not doable now, try this as a backup plan. Offer to write a statement of how DEI is an integral component for achieving the corporate vision and mission that you can tag on below the vision and mission statement. The goal is to connect DEI directly to the organization's guidepost.

Step 4 – If your company has stated values, look for ways to add DEI to each of the values. Again, if possible, offer to re-write the values to maintain their core meaning while adding DEI as appropriate. If that's not an option, offer to write how DEI is an essential element of each of the core values.

Step 5 – During the strategic planning process, anchor your recommendations for the inclusion of DEI in the overall strategy. Also, ensure DEI is part of the plans of each major sector of your company. Work directly with the CEO to make sure DEI is part of the top-level management strategy, and then work with each direct report of the CEO to ensure DEI is part of their plan to support the CEO strategy.

While taking these steps may require a lot of work and boldness, they will ensure that your DEI efforts are entirely woven into the fabric of your organization.

Tip 2 – Become Your CEO's Trusted Advisor

Being a trusted advisor is not the same as reporting to your CEO. CEOs have a lot of people reporting to them who I would not categorize as their trusted advisors. As a former Vistage Chair and speaker, I had the rare opportunity to meet with hundreds of CEOs. Vistage is a peer mentoring membership organization for CEOs and business owners. The person who provides one-on-one coaching to the CEOs and chairs their peer discussion groups is called a group Chair. "Everybody in my company wants something from me. They all have their agendas linked to their silos or personal needs. I'm the only one who focuses totally on the big picture." That was a common statement I heard from CEOs I spoke with when they talked about their roles and relationships with others in their organizations.

Those CEOs might have a team that included HR, operations, accounting, and legal leaders, but none of these would be categorized by them as fully trusted advisors. With each one, the CEO had to balance the overall objectives of the big picture against their perception of the other's agendas. That's why they loved their peer groups and their group Chairs. The group Chair was there for one reason only: to support the progress of the CEO's agenda. Likewise, the peer CEOs from non-competitive organizations contributed to their success. The Chair and peer group were the CEOs trusted advisors. This doesn't mean that a senior leader in the organization cannot rise to the level of their CEO's trusted advisor. It just means that their leadership title alone as head of this or that silo, does not automatically confer trusted advisor status on anyone.

One definition of a trusted advisor is someone who plays a crucial role in achieving the client's goals in the client's best interest. You do not need to be a direct report to fulfill this role, although that can help by providing more frequent access. Your title is not that important either, although this helps with perceptions of value. Here's what you do need. You DO need to provide your CEO with sound advice based on your broad experience and knowledge of what's in the CEO's best interest. In short, you need to secure the CEO's respect for your knowledge and trust.

For a CDO, my research shows the essential elements of becoming your CEO's trusted advisor are knowing the organization's business, knowing your CEO's objectives, and providing advice that helps the CEO leverage DEI to meet their objectives. With this in mind, here are some steps you can take to become your CEO's trusted advisor.

Step 1–Learn your company's core business. I don't mean just reading annual reports or books on the industry. I mean, REALLY get to know the business. Do a ride-along with a front-line professional. Offer to shadow people in your operations. And also, get acquainted with the company's back-office processes like HR, Accounting, etc. But make sure you nail those core business factors.

Step 2–Find out exactly how your current state of DEI impacts your core business. If you're a for-profit, how does your current state of DEI affect your ability to serve the largest possible market? How does it give or deprive your company of inside track clients' and prospects' information? If you're a non-profit, how does it impact your ability to carry out your mission?

Don't rely solely on general statistics or quotes. Those are good for bolstering a position based on company-specific facts.

Step 3–Find out your CEO's top long-term and short-term goals. The easiest and most direct way to do this is to schedule a meeting with your CEO. Tell them how you believe a targeted DEI effort can support them in meeting their goals. Convey how this meeting aims to get their direct perspectives to focus DEI efforts on the areas most important to the CEO.

By the way, if you are told to meet with the CHRO or some other role subordinate to the CEO, mention that you plan to meet with this person and other direct reports of the CEO. However, emphasize that you want to ensure that your efforts focus on the big picture aspects. To that end, you would appreciate 30 minutes of their time.

If you still get pushed to meeting with HR or some other subordinate role at this point, I recommend you consider that perhaps this is not the best company for you. This is especially true if you want to be a CDO that significantly impacts your organization.

I'm not saying your role must report to the CEO. (That is, of course, the ideal arrangement). However, you need to have at minimum the CEO's input, support, and access to their ear. Otherwise, you will not be running a strategic practice that can support the company as it moves through our disruptive future.

Step 4 – Assuming you get the meeting with the CEO, come prepared to interview them. Ask questions like, what is your long-term goal for the business? What do you see as your most significant opportunities, and conversely, what are your biggest obstacles?

As you listen to the CEO's responses, note where DEI can play a role in seizing opportunities and removing obstacles. If you've done your homework on the business before this meeting, these ideas will pop out. Share them broadly with your CEO.

Step 5 – Before leaving this meeting, offer to participate in the annual strategic planning meeting. This should be both your offer and your ask. This is your opportunity to hitch your efforts to the company's annual strategy and embed DEI into the yearly plan.

Having a seat at the table and reporting to the CEO are all great objectives for CDOs that want to have a meaningful impact on the company strategy. But the most important thing is for you to achieve the status of a trusted advisor.

Tip 3 – Integrate Your Practice Across the Organization

Another critical success factor in addressing challenges and opportunities in a complex, disruptive business environment is having a well-structured operation. Some organizations have this down pat. Here's what I've found in my research a well-structured nimble DEI effort includes. ERGs are formed, chartered, funded, and managed using a fair, transparent process. Every single ERG has at least one Executive Sponsor. These Executive Sponsors are direct reports to the CEO. If the company maintains relationships with the outside boards of community groups, the appropriate ERG Executive Sponsor will hold that seat for the company. So, for example, if the company maintains a board relationship with a women's non-profit, the Executive Sponsor of the Women's ERG will sit on that outside board.

Executive Sponsors are also members of the Corporate Diversity Council, which includes other vital representatives who are leaders of the organization's primary function areas (E.g., HR, Operations, etc.). Finally, a smaller group of the senior leaders form a Diversity Steering Committee, Chaired by the CEO. In some organizations, the CEO Chairs the Corporate Diversity Council directly. This, in effect, makes the council both an advisory and a decision-making body.

Because these components of the DEI effort and governance are woven together in an integrated structure, you'll find it easier to maintain alignment. You can also communicate up, down, and across this structure quickly. Within the structure, the governance role of the head of DEI is clearly defined. For example, relative to ERGs, the CDO's role is to support the efforts through a structure that enables good communication and coordination throughout the organization. Another component of the CDO role relative to ERGs is to help upskill group leaders and executive sponsors. (More on this in upcoming tips).

In the case of the Corporate Diversity Council, the CDO can Chair this group, unless it's Chaired by the CEO and acts as a hybrid Council/Steering Committee. When serving as the Chair of the council, the CDO's role is to maintain the focus on DEI issues that impact the organization's interest. Since the ERG Executive Sponsors are part of this group, the voices of the ERGs are also in the room. A powerful way to Chair these meetings to get to solid recommendations is to drive them with questions like:

1. What's working? What are we doing in the organization relative to DEI that produces a positive result in the workforce, workplace, and marketplace that is of value to our business?
2. Why are these things working? Consider the elements that have yielded your success to date?
3. What's not perfect yet? Where is the lack of effective DEI creating an obstacle or preventing the company from seizing a workforce, workplace, or marketplace opportunity?
4. What resources or actions do we need to address this obstacle or opportunity?
5. Of all the suggestions, which ones are the top ones that the group would like to consider for recommendations?

Suppose the Council meets monthly, and the Steering Committee meets quarterly. In that case, The CDO can combine and finetune the findings and recommendations of the council and present them to the Steering Committee. Adopted recommendations can be forwarded for action by the CDO to the appropriate process owners. The CDO can also report back to the council the decisions of the Steering Committee. And voila! That's an integrated process.

Here are some steps you can take to create an integrated and organized DEI practice if you don't have one.

Step 1 – Create an organization chart for your DEI efforts. Include all your ERGs, the Executive Sponsors, Council members, and decision-makers up to the CEO. Now scrutinize it and ask yourself the following questions:

1. Is there a clear charter with roles and responsibilities outlined for ERG leaders? Are the means by which ERGs get formed, supported, funded, and managed fair and transparent?
2. Does each of your ERGs have an Executive Sponsor that reports to the CEO?
3. Does the Executive Sponsor also cover external groups of interest to the company that focuses on the same dimension of diversity that their ERG represents?
4. Does the Executive Sponsor have a seat and a voice in the Corporate Diversity Council?
5. Is the CEO connected to the DEI process? Is the CEO either the Chair of the Council or heading a DEI Steering Committee?

Step 2 – Fix any broken links within or between the ERG and the Council. In other words, take care of items 1 through 4 in the above list, before you loop in the CEO. You want to present your CEO and the Steering Committee with a finetuned execution and advisory machine.

Step 3 – Recommend a Steering Committee to the CEO. Explain how you will develop the agenda and create all the materials for this short decision-making meeting. Remember, the most valuable thing a CEO has is their time. The plan for this meeting can be fed directly from the output of your Council meetings. Here's a simple format I've found works very well in my research.

- First, open the meeting with a progress report highlighting all the areas where the company is succeeding in driving value to the workforce, workplace, and marketplace, through its DEI efforts.
- Next, go through each area that presents opportunities for improvement and the Council's recommendation for review and approval. Be specific in this segment. One model I found works well here is the one referred to by the acronym STAR. Present the SITUATION, followed by the TARGET objective and ACTIONS recommended, and close with the expected RESULTS. (Ideally, this will include return on investment numbers from Finance and Accounting). The Steering Committee, chaired by the CEO, can then intelligently deliberate on each recommendation based on the facts.
- Once all the decisions are made and recorded, the meeting can close.

And that's it.

There are certainly elements of DEI that are supported by passionate leadership. And there is undoubtedly value to being an excellent external spokesperson for the company on these critical topics. But unless a CDO has a well-oiled, highly integrated machine governing the process, tangible, measurable success will not come. And in the current and increasing state of disruption, the substance is becoming more critical than just PR and marketing.

Tip 4 – Get Involved in Your Company's Digital Revolution

According to a 2019 Mercer report, forty percent of companies use AI to screen and assess candidates [(2)]. Some see AI as a tool to remove unconscious bias. As I mentioned earlier, sixty-three percent of the senior human resources executives, responding to my 2020 survey, thought the adoption of AI would automatically take human bias out of screening job candidates. But that's not true. AI often has the same biases as the people who build and train it.

An increasing number of companies are now using text and voice chat to conduct recorded screening. An AI later reviews these recorded interviews and assesses the candidates using voice tones and facial expression analysis. As noted earlier in this book, AI usage is not limited to hiring within HR. According to one article, eighty-three percent of US companies are now using some form of AI in their various HR processes [3]. Furthermore, the use of AI is not just spreading inside HR. It's also spreading rapidly throughout all your organizational processes, including those that touch your marketplace operations and relationships. Right now, thirty-seven percent of organizations use forms of AI throughout their company. That number is expected to grow. Investors believe that by 2027 the AI market will grow to $267 billion US dollars and that AI will contribute another 15.7 trillion to the global economy by 2030 ([4]).

So, what's the bottom line here? Here are three facts followed by a conclusion. First, AI is rapidly taking over many of the workforce, workplace, and marketplace decisions that used to be made by people. Second, many DEI leaders, steeped in the traditional work of DEI, are focused on bias and micro-aggressions among people. We are spending billions in diversity and unconscious bias training. Meanwhile, we're ignoring these biased digital decision-making machines that are taking over many HR and business functions. It's as if the profession were suffering from attentional blindness that makes viewers of the famous basketball players and gorilla video, not see the gorilla. Third, suppose DEI leaders delay getting involved a bit longer. In that case, they will likely be surrounded by inequitable and biased systems that shape the next generation of the workforce, workplace, and marketplace. The conclusion is simple. DEI leaders need to get involved in AI now.

The good news is that you don't need to be a technical expert to guide and manage the deployment of AI systems. You just need to be plugged into the right places in the process. Here are three basic steps to get engaged in this process.

Step 1 – Find out if your company has an AI/technology governance committee. AI/technology governance committees generate AI adoption and usage policies to ensure the organization's legal, ethical, and transparent use of AI. Typically, these committees come up with AI purchasing and usage policies. These policies often contain anti-discrimination and anti-bias language. Sometimes, these groups use anti-bias statements, which we talked about earlier in one of the ten ERG leadership tips.

According to Venjara of ADP, the best way to find out if you have an existing committee is to go to the head of your IT department. You can also check with Legal. Generally, these two groups will have seats on that committee.

Step 2 – If there is an existing AI/technology governance committee, ask to join. Find out what policies and guidelines already exist. If bias is not addressed in the policies, lobby for its inclusion. If anti-bias statements are missing, lobby for those to be created and used. Also, find out if any parts of the company, like HR, have brought AI or other technologies under the committee's radar and bring those to the table for review.

If your company does not have an AI/technology governance committee, offer to form one. Start by talking to legal about the exposure to the company presented by potential AI biases in hiring, promotion, and client relationships. Bring in representatives from the IT department and other parts of the company. Put together a policy and statements if you don't have these, and get them approved, adopted, and communicated.

Step 3 – Assemble your sub-committee comprised of leaders of your ERGs. Share AI and technology policies and statements with your ERG leaders so they can review them with their members and give you input you can finetune and bring back to the AI/technology committee. This enables you to bring to the table the voice and concerns of the various underrepresented communities.

As you can see, to get involved in your company's digital revolution, you don't need to be a technical expert. Your value is in the expertise you already bring to include the perspectives and voices of many communities and your experience with addressing bias and inequity.

Tip 5 – Build a House for Diversity

In his seminal 1999 book, ***Building a House for Diversity*** [(5)], author and diversity thought-leader R. Roosevelt Thomas, used a simple fable worth revisiting. It's an insightful fable about a giraffe and an elephant. Here is my abridged version.

Once, in a small suburban community, a giraffe had a new home built to his family's specifications. It was a wonderful house for giraffes, with soaring ceilings and tall doorways. High windows ensured maximum light and good views while protecting the family's privacy.

Narrow hallways saved valuable space without compromising convenience. So well done was the house that it won the National Giraffe Home of the Year Award. The homeowners were very proud.

One day the giraffe, working in his state-of-the-art woodshop in the basement, happened to look out of the window. Coming down the street was an elephant. "I know him," he thought. He's an excellent woodworker, too. I think I'll invite him in to see my new shop and work on some projects with me." So, the giraffe poked his head out the window and invited the elephant to join him. The elephant was delighted the giraffe was inviting him in. So, he walked up to the door and waited for it to open. "Come in; come in," the giraffe said to the elephant.

But immediately they encountered a problem. While the elephant could get his head in the door, he could go no farther. "It's a good thing we made this door expandable to accommodate my woodshop equipment," the giraffe said. "Give me a minute while I take care of our problem." He removed some bolts and panels to let the elephant enter.

The two acquaintances were exchanging woodworking stories when the giraffe's wife leaned her head down the stairs and called her husband: "Telephone, dear." "I'd better take that upstairs in the den," the giraffe told the elephant. "Please make yourself at home."

The elephant looked around, saw a half-finished piece of work on the lathe table in the far corner, and decided to explore it further. As he moved through the doorway that led to the shop, he heard an ominous crunch. He backed out, scratching his head. "Maybe I'll just join the giraffe upstairs," he thought. But as he started up the stairs, he heard the stairs begin to crack. So, he jumped off and fell back against the wall, and it began to crumble. So, he sat there disheveled and dismayed as the giraffe came down the stairs. "What on earth is happening here?" the giraffe asked in amazement. "I was trying to make myself at home," the elephant said. The giraffe looked around and said, "Okay, I see the problem. The doorway is too narrow, and the floors, walls, and stairs can't support your weight, so we'll have to make you smaller. There's an aerobics studio near here. If you'd take some classes there, we could get you down to size." "Maybe," the elephant said, not looking very convinced. Then added, "But to tell you the truth, I'm not sure a house designed for a giraffe will ever really work for an elephant, not unless there are some major changes."

During my years in DEI, I have heard many talk about these changes Dr. Thomas was referring to, being about inclusion. In other words, before you can bring in diversity, you have to prepare to be inclusive. I've always disagreed with that interpretation. Here's why. Verna Myers' famous quote states, "Diversity is being invited to the party. Inclusion is being asked to dance." The elephant was invited to the party, so put a check next to diversity. The elephant was also being asked to dance, so we can put a check next to inclusion. So, what was missing? Why couldn't the elephant fully participate? The elephant gives us the answer. "I'm not sure a house designed for a giraffe will ever really work for an elephant, not unless there are some major changes." This is about design, which is entirely about equity.

Equity, unfortunately, as Minal Bopaiah tells us in her book, **Equity: How to Design Organizations Where Everyone Thrives** [6], is the often-ignored element of the DEI effort. Equity requires DEI leaders to push the organization to redesign or build new systems that support diversity and make inclusion more possible and meaningful. In Dr. Thomas' story, he wasn't asking the readers to find ways to invite more elephants into the house that was ill-suited for them. He was asking the reader to consider re-building the house to accommodate elephants and giraffes.

The giraffes in our world are the straight White male of the 1950s, with a stay-at-home wife, who took care of all the caring duties of a family and home. The entire company "house" of policies, procedures, and practices has been built to support the best performance out of this group. This thinking influenced everything from what's covered in reimbursement policies, such as transportation to meetings and drinks with prospects, to what is not, such as a babysitter. We can add pay structure, benefits coverage, and a host of other items to this list. All of these have been designed for our proverbial "giraffes," the straight White male of the 1950s with a stay-at-home wife. Everyone else is an elephant. Everyone else is trying to figure out how to do their best and succeed in this house that was not built for them. And that's where you, as a DEI leader, have a role in building a house for diversity. That is the role of DEI as the champion of equity.

So how can you start focusing on the E in DEI and start pushing towards building a house for diversity in your organization? Here are a few bold steps you can take.

Step 1 – Start examining every system and policy in your company using the following three questions:

1. Who does this support and benefit?
2. Who does this leave out or inconvenience?
3. What can we do to create equal opportunity?

Let's look at two quick examples. Suppose you have an expense reimbursement policy covering travel, lodging, and entertainment incurred in client prospect meetings that do not cover babysitting. As you go through the questions, you can immediately see how such a policy disadvantages working mothers with a toddler in sales. A quick fix would be to revise the policy to include babysitting costs incurred relative to attending client meetings.

Another example would be your religious Holiday policy. Does your company close for Christmas as a paid holiday, but people of other faiths must take vacation days? Perhaps you can remedy that by only including secular holidays in your general holiday schedule and letting team members take faith-based time off out of a personal day pool.

Step 2 – Share policy and practice documents with your ERG leaders and ask them to review them with their members and give you feedback.

Before asking them to engage in this work, invest in giving them a general education on the topic of equity. You can use the abridged elephant and giraffe fable to provide them with context. Next, share the policy and practice information and ask them to give you feedback on how components of the current organization's "house-structure" are working or not working for them. This is an excellent way to "crowdsource" your review of the opportunities for more equity and to come up with solutions.

Step 3 – Likewise, look at the policies and practices you use to engage with clients. Similar to the Pizza giant that failed to build an online presence that could serve the blind pizza-buying community, your organization may be ignoring market share. Remember, the organizational house is not only built to employ the giraffe, but many are also made only exclusively to sell and serve giraffes. Given the demographic shifts happening locally and globally, that could mean your company will be serving a shrinking marketplace. Unless, of course, you help the organization rebuild its house into one that can serve the growing market of elephants too.

By building a house for diversity, you will be advancing your organization's ability to be more successful today and in the coming decades of disruption.

Tip 6 – Develop Your ERG Executive Sponsors

There is a common fallacy in our thinking. It makes us believe that because someone is a senior leader considered exceptionally brilliant at their job, they will be competent at everything. In my experience and research, nothing could be further from the truth. This is especially true regarding the ability that executives will bring to their role as ERG executive sponsors.

In an article penned by my friend and colleague, Neddy Perez, a highly experienced CDO who served in many high-profile companies, she talks about the importance of executive sponsors. Her article focuses on the importance of these sponsors to disability ERGs. But Perez's comments apply to the sponsor of any ERG. She states, "Executive Sponsors are critical to the success of ERGs/BRGs." She continued to explain that they serve as advocates to help advance understanding about disabilities and pay special attention. Then she goes on to say, "They also serve as a coach to the employees who have volunteered to serve on the leadership committee of the ERG/BRG (7)." I can tell you with absolute certainty based on research, countless interviews, and experience that most executives are not skilled coaches.

In my many conversations with senior leaders, I've found that they often confuse being directive or mentoring based on their experience with being a coach. That's when I point out that mentoring is a process where the mentor shares their experience with a mentee. On the other hand, I explain that as a coach, you can bring out and help develop talents and abilities in your coachees beyond those possessed by you. After I put them through a one-hour coaching program, I often hear comments like, "I never knew what coaching was about or that it could be so simple yet powerful." And "In addition to using this with ERG leaders, I'm going to use this with all my team members." The bottom line is that coaching is a skill many of them don't have, and they simply won't just get it because they are brilliant. But with a bit of training, they can quickly get up to speed. The same is true for other roles we expect these executive sponsors to fill. For example, in some organizations, ERG executive sponsors are expected to:

- Find opportunities to leverage the group to address significant opportunities or challenges in the organization.
- Scout for emerging talent in the group.
- Provide business guidance to group leaders.
- Serve as liaison to external communities that align the group with businesses interest.
- Etc.

None of the skills required to do these comes automatically to smart people. These skills need to be learned. Here are a few steps you can take to start setting your ERG Executive Sponsors up for success:

Step 1 – Identify what you would like Executive Sponsors to do for your ERGs and organization. Write it out using a performance result description format that includes the following elements:

- What results are you looking for out of a successful Executive Sponsor?

- □ What specific skills and services will they need to employ to produce these results?

Step 2- Identify the Executive Sponsor training curriculum you will use to bring all your executive sponsors up to speed. This could be a combination of instructor-led and videos. Make this part of your Executive Sponsor onboarding process, along with information about time commitments and other expectations for the role.

Step 3 – Periodically revisit your training program and make sure that it continues to support the development of the skills and tools needed to address your critical objectives for this role.

Executive Sponsors, just like ERG leaders, are part of your DEI efforts' extended leadership team. I urge you to invest in their development.

Tip 7 – Develop Your ERG Leaders

We've all seen what my years of research have told me. The leader of an ERG is one of the key factors behind an ERG's success. Just think about the impact on one of your floundering ERGs when a new vibrant, highly skilled leader took the helm.

Unfortunately, passion and desire do not automatically confer skills in creating a powerful unifying vision, organizing, engaging, and mobilizing a group of member volunteers. That requires intentional development and training. Over the past half a century since ERGs first appeared, the only sources for that development were:

1. They attended a company in-person leadership training program with a high per-seat cost. Also, these programs were designed for formal leaders of employee groups and not leaders of volunteer organizations like ERGs, so not all elements were easily applicable.
2. They attended a customized in-person or online instructor-led program with a similarly high per-seat cost for ERG leaders.
3. They were sent to an ERG leader resource group conference with a few instructive panels and speakers. This, on average, could cost your company between $1,200 to $2,000 per person, based

on conference entry fees, travel, meals, and lodging expenses. Companies did not send all their ERG Chairs to these programs.

I'm sure it won't surprise you to learn that many ERG leaders back then, never received any training. It was simply too expensive and required a big chunk of time off from the ERG leader's regular job. But, with more online programs becoming available in recent years, that's changed. There's a lot that you can do to put together an affordable targeted training program today, using free TedTalks and other outlets. I would especially recommend turning your ERG leaders on to the ERG PowerTalk podcast. This is a free program sponsored by the CDO PowerCircle that offers ERG leaders over $100,000 worth of free training and inspiration. Here are just a few of the thought-leaders who've shared their insights on the podcast:

- Dr. Ed. Hubbard, President, and CEO of Hubbard & Hubbard, on how to calculate your ERGs ROI.
- Howard Ross, Founder of Cook Ross, and author of several leading books on social justice and bias on building ERGs that support members and allies.
- Dr. Inga Carboni, an expert on organizational analysis and author of Connect the Dots, on how ERGs can grow their influence and measure their impact through the science of organizational analysis.
- Doz Thornton, former President of the Georgia Chapter of the National Speakers Association and a CEO speaking coach, on putting together powerful ERG presentations in record time with little effort.
- Julie Kantor, founder, and former President and CEO of TwoMentor, on how to rapidly set up a powerful ERG member mentoring program.
- Kelly Newman, Lead Facilitator for Blue EQ on how ERG leaders can develop their emotional intelligence.
- Simone Morris, author of the Power of Owning Your Career, on leveraging ERG leadership roles to grow as a leader and future executive.

- Dr. Kim Olver, Licensed Clinical Professional Counselor, and expert on Choice Theory, on how to expand your appeal to members and engage more people in your efforts.
- Bob Rosen, a trusted CEO advisor, New York Times Bestselling Author, and an expert in healthy leadership on leading healthy ERGs.
- Dr. Theresa Welbourne, Professor of Business and President and CEO of eePulse, on how ERGs energize their organizations.
- Stephen Krempl, former VP at Starbucks and Yum University, and current CEO of a coaching organization, called StandingOut/W3 on getting the favorable attention of senior leadership.

All your ERG leaders need to do to access this treasure trove of insights and inspiration is go to the online page referenced by this link https://linktr.ee/Joesan58 and pick their favorite listening platform. As noted in tip number 8 of Chapter 5, they can bundle listening to the podcast with other daily activities to save time while building their leadership muscle.

Another useful low-cost tool you can give your ERG leaders to help them quickly find practical ways to step up their ERG practice performance is to provide them with a copy of **SuperCharge Your ERGs: 18 Tips to Power-up Your ERG/BRG Strategy**. This small book contains my distilled decade of research into what makes some ERGs outstanding. The tips are easy to understand and implement. You can pick up a copy of the paperback for $8.95 on Amazon or the Kindle version for $5.95. Considering the value of the information in this small book, it offers a significant return on your investment [(8)].

So, here are a few steps you can take to put together a quick ERG leadership development program.

Step 1 – Open a fresh spreadsheet and label it ERG Leadership Development Program sheet. Here in the first column, list all the things you would like your ERG leaders to support through their groups. In the column to the immediate right of that list, write down all the skills your ERG leaders would need to deliver on the objectives you listed in the first column. Next, go one more column to the right, and list next to each required skill, a learning source for acquiring that skill—for example, the podcast, a book, a TEDTalk, etc. I would recommend getting a partner from your training department with instructional design training to help you with this and the next step.

Step 2 – With your instructional design partner, put together a learning curriculum for year one ERG leaders. You can also put together a year two or ongoing learning curriculum for your ERG leaders to follow, after completing their year one Bootcamp.

Step 3 – Give this to all your current ERG leaders, and then make it part of your new ERG leadership onboarding process.

Training ERG leaders can significantly benefit you and your DEI practice, especially in these turbulent times and going forward. A little investment in the effort here will pay dividends to you for years to come.

Tip 8 – Free Your ERGs from Corporate Friction

Want to know the number one thing that slows down your ERG leaders and keeps them from doing more for you and your organization? The answer is "Corporate Friction." Those are my words. Here are some of the things I've heard from ERG leaders that I collectively put under the label "Corporate Friction."

"It takes forever to get a program announcement approved. First, we must send it to Legal, HR, and the Office of DEI. Then we must answer email questions. Next, we have to follow up slow responses by people who place our request for a review at the bottom of their to-do pile."

"My manager has no idea what I do in my ERG. She often questions whether I should skip these meetings and focus more on my important work in her department."

"Every time we invite a speaker, they need to be vetted by various parts of our organization. The process can take weeks."

"I need to make a budget request for every program and wait for weeks to get approval before moving forward. Sometimes I have to follow up several times just to get a status on my request for review."

I'm sure we all recognize this as part of the slow bureaucratic processes that are part of corporate life. Even at the most senior levels, most of us don't have a choice but to live with it. If you have a job within a company, you have to deal with all the "Corporate Friction" that makes doing your job seem like you're swimming against a powerful current. Smart organizations try to take as much of this out as possible, to increase efficiencies, but a lot of it still often remains embedded deep within the company. But when it comes to ERG leaders, there is a different set of dynamics.

If you are in a job that requires you to produce a particular result that forces you to face several frustrating hurdles, put in your way by corporate bureaucracy, you have no choice but to plow forward and deal with it. On the other hand, if you have a busy full-time job and are engaging in activity on behalf of the organization as a volunteer, you have another choice. Don't engage. Stop the presses and stand pat. And unfortunately, that is what often happens based on my research.

"I would like to do this, but I already have a lot of stress from my regular job, and I don't want to load myself with more" is a common complaint I've heard over the years. Sometimes, you might have one or two ERG leaders that soldier on while others stand back, but these brave few often get burnt out and discouraged. So, what's the solution?

The answer is to remove as much of this "Corporate Friction" as possible for these volunteer roles. Here are some of the things some organizations do to that end, which I've come across in my research.

- □ The Office of DEI prepares and shares a document with the managers of ERG leaders that explains what the ERGs do that adds value to the company. This document outlines the role of the ERG and the ERG leader. These documents also list all the benefits ERG leaders bring to their departments and managers.
- □ The Office of DEI works with the ERGs to obtain approval for standard templates and art for announcements and slides. They also get preapproval for a bench of speaker candidates.
- □ The Office of DEI works with the ERG leaders to determine budgetary needs for the year and secure the funding. This funding is then used to pay for projects and programs throughout the year, without the ERG leader having to shepherd each request through a long, frustrating process.

Here are some steps you can follow to remove as much "Corporate Friction" as possible from your volunteer ERG leaders.

Step 1 – Have either you or a member of your Office of DEI, sit with your ERG leaders to find out what slows them down and blocks their progress. Share some elements of your own frustration with the company bureaucracy to prime the discussion pump.

Step 2 – Brainstorm ways you and your team can proactively address and remove these obstacles. Perhaps can create Frequently Ask Question (FAQ) guides, templates, budget pre-approvals, pre-cleared speakers, etc. Put templates into online repositories where they are easy to access and use.

Step 3. Encourage ERG leaders to report obstacles to your Office of DEI as they come up. Make it a point to continuously look for ways to clear the path and make it easier for these passionate volunteers to do their best.

The more obstacles you remove, the more you will reap the rewards of performance and results from your ERGs.

Tip 9 – Build Tomorrow's Pool of Leaders

One of the marks of being a true leader is the creation of other leaders. There is a quote about this attributed to Tom Peter. Peters is an American business expert and author of several management books, including the 1982 bestseller, "In Search of Excellence." He states, "Leaders don't create followers, they create more leaders." Why is this especially important for DEI leaders today? Because if you create more followers in your team, you increase your workload. This slows down your entire organization's ability to react to a changing environment full of disruption. On the other hand, the more leaders you create, the faster and nimbler you become.

Additionally, as a DEI leader, you want to ensure that tomorrow's leadership better reflects the communities being led. You want to have people at the top of the house that possess and understand the perspectives and needs of the increasingly diverse workforce, workplace, and marketplace. By seeding a more diverse perspective into your organization's leadership at all levels, you increase the company's ability to recognize and quickly respond to a variety of opportunities and challenges.

And a great way to accomplish these goals is by turning your ERGs into leadership development engines. This is not just armchair speculation. In a 2015 study by a CDO association I chaired, we found that organizations with the highest performance levels were outpacing others in leveraging their ERGs to develop leaders.

Further research I conducted through countless interviews over the past decade with CDOs, including those in the CDO PowerCircle, has uncovered some specific ways that the DEI Offices of these leading organizations use their ERGs to develop more leaders. Here are just five ways. One, they have a process to identify skills needed by people leading their ERGs. One way to do this is to have the CDO or someone from the Office of DEI or the ERG executive sponsor meet with the person's supervisor. The purpose of this meeting is to discuss the opportunities for learning various skills, such as presenting, project management, influencing, etc., and to focus on a specific area of individual developmental needs. Two, they create a learning partnership that lets the budding leader observe a good role model of the behavior they want the developing leader to learn. Three, after an appropriate amount of time watching the role model, they get the budding leader to start practicing the new behavior within the safety of the ERG. Four, they have the developing leader coached by their Executive Sponsor and other more advanced peers to increase their mastery of the skill further. And finally, five, they work with the developing leader's supervisor to encourage bringing these skills into their work, outside the ERG.

In some organizations, the Office of DEI increases this partnership between DEI and the leadership development function by selecting people deemed high potentials from the various demographic communities, to head up ERGs. This, like any other process, has its pluses and minuses. It does, however, tie leadership development to a ready-made process for gaining on-the-ground experience exercising new leadership skills. In other organizations, the Office of DEI increases the visibility of emerging leaders coming out of this ERG development engine, by placing them into short-term shadowing roles with senior leaders in various parts of the organization. In one such program, I took part in years ago at Siemens, an emerging leader would be sent to shadow an executive for a week or two. The emerging leader would participate in all the host executive's non-confidential meetings during this time. She would also meet with the executives' direct reports to learn more about the challenges and opportunities of the hosting team. Pre-shadowing and post-shadowing briefings were held during scheduled meals between the executive and the emerging leader. The entire cost of this program was a small amount of travel, lodging, and meal expenses. The returns were huge in generating visibility and opportunity for freshly minted leaders.

In my writing and speeches, I've often shared a story titled "Acres of Diamonds," from a book by Russell Conwell, published in 1890. It's a story about a man who sold his farm and home to go unsuccessfully looking for diamonds in a far-off land. The man never realized that the land he once owned and sold, littered with a bounty of almost colorless transparent stones with a light yellowish to brownish tint, was indeed a rich field of diamonds in the rough. With a bit of effort, many Offices of DEI will find massive deposits of "future leaders in the rough" from all demographic communities sitting in their midst. Your ERGs contain all the tools you need to polish these future leaders into brilliant corporate gemstones. I invite you to follow the steps of high-performance companies and start leveraging your ERGs to shape and polish your leadership treasures.

Here are a few steps you can take to start revving up your ERG leadership development engine.

Step 1 – Meet with your organization's talent development team to learn more about their current practices. Look for opportunities to partner with them, to provide leadership development vehicles for your ERG leaders.

Step 2 – Schedule a meeting between your Office of DEI and the ERG Executive Sponsors to explore ways to develop the leadership skills of your ERG leaders. Share some of the examples in this tip and see which combination might work best for your company.

Step 3 – Meet with your ERG leaders and share your plans for turning their term as ERG leaders into an opportunity to develop them for more significant leadership roles within the organization. Also, encourage ERG leaders to scout for their successors and invite them to join you in being leaders who create more leaders.

By running your ERGs as engines that create more leaders from all your diverse communities, you will be further enabling your organization to thrive in today and tomorrow's complex and disruptive environment.

Tip 10 – Build a Powerful Organization-Wide DEI Team

So far, in earlier tips, we've talked about developing individual members of your extended DEI team. The extended team includes your Office of DEI personnel, ERG Executive Sponsors, ERG Leaders, liaisons, and allies. But while developing the individuals that make up a team does make them individually more effective; it does not necessarily result in better teamwork. Here's why.

In 2012, Google embarked on an initiative code-named Project Aristotle. They studied hundreds of their teams to figure out why some stumbled while others soared. Before conducting this study, leaders at Google, like in many organizations, believed that the best teams result when you put together people at the top of their class. The idea was simple. Put together the smartest MBAs, engineers, and a high-flying Ph.D., and voila! You would have the perfect high-performing team. That was the hypothesis based on their gut feeling [(9)].

Set on this image of the "perfect-super-team," senior leaders at Google put Abeer Dubey, director of Google's People Analytics division, in charge of the project named Project Aristotle. Dubey dutifully gathered some of the company's best statisticians, organizational psychologists, sociologists, engineers, and researchers. One of these researchers was Julia Rosovsky, Google's people analytics manager. Over two years, this team studied 180 Google teams, conducted 200-plus interviews, and analyzed over 250 different team attributes. Unfortunately, they did not find a clear pattern of personal characteristics that, brought together, would create the sought-after "super-team."

It wasn't until 2014 when the Google team started considering that perhaps the hypothesis of the super-team made up of the best people, might be wrong. At this point, they found a new line of thinking that led to the secret of creating superior teams. This new line of thought focused on the intangible connections between people known as "group norms." These include the traditions, behavioral standards, and unwritten rules governing how people work together. With this new lens and some additional direction from a study on collective intelligence by a group of psychologists from Carnegie Mellon, MIT, and Union College, Project Aristotle's researchers went back to the drawing board to comb their data for unspoken customs.

Here are the five essential characteristics shared by superior teams that they found, as outlined by Rozovsky in Google's Re: Work website. One, the team members have psychological safety. Team members feel they can take risks without fear of being negatively judged and embarrassed by other team members. Two, the team members can depend on each other. Team members feel they can count on each other to do high-quality work and keep time commitments. Three, the team has structure and clarity. There are clear goals, roles, and plans for the team. Four, the team's work is meaningful. Team members are working on something personally important to them. And five, the team members believe their work has a beneficial impact. Team members believe that the work they're doing matters. In the end, when it came to producing superior results from a highly coordinated team, these elements of social connection mattered more than the individual capabilities of the team members [(10)].

In my research and work with CEOs and CDOs, I've found that the leader is in the best position to bring these five elements of success to a team. That leader can be a formal department head, the volunteer committee chair, or a meeting host. Here's a simple example of how I put these conditions in place for meetings I ran with CEOs and CDOs.

First, I would open the meeting with rules to put psychological safety in place. At a minimum, these rules included: One, Be Respectful, and Non-Judgmental—no judgment on suggestions or questions posed by participants. Just because I disagree with your idea or way of thinking doesn't make either of us right or wrong. We just have different viewpoints. Two, Be Present. All participants are expected to give the discussion their full and undivided attention. And three, I own the structure, but participants own the content. In other words, I would drive the phases of the discussion. For example, I would reinforce more clarifying questions until an opportunity or challenge that was under review was fully understood, before letting the group move to offer solutions. I would not, however, critique or modify their clarifying questions or comments. Second, I informed participants that we were going to take turns collectively listening to, examining, and brainstorming potential solutions for each other's opportunity or challenge. This made group participants inter-dependent on solutions, instead of just looking to me for answers. Third, I established the goals of the meeting. In these meetings, this was to help all the participants resolve their most significant opportunities and challenges. This put a clear group objective in place. Fourth, since the meeting was focused on THEIR challenges and opportunities, it was personally important to them as participants. And finally, fifth, during my initial questions about the challenges each of them presented, I would ask the participants to state why this opportunity or challenge was of such high priority to them. This fixed in their minds and the minds of the other participants, that the topics we were covering were of high impact. As you can see, even in a short-term team that gets together for the occasional meeting, it's not that difficult for you as a leader to add a few key ingredients to boost team performance.

As the leader of your company's DEI effort comprising an Office of DEI members and an extended team of volunteer Executive Sponsors and ERG leaders, this can be a big part of your ability to mobilize these team members for high impact. Here are a few steps you can take to start doing this right away.

Step 1 – Use DEI and ERG meetings and summits to bring together your various team members. Many of the qualities of trust and safety needed to create super-teams can be developed by getting people to know each other better. Studies, like the one led by Hunter Gehlbach and Maureen E. Brinkworth, detailed in a paper titled **Creating Birds of Similar Feathers: Leveraging Similarity to Improve Teacher-Student Relationships and Academic Achievement** [11] show how engineered familiarity results in improved partnership. Try using a warmup exercise like the "I am from" poem to see how quickly your participants will get personally comfortable with each other. For instructions on preparing and running this insightful exercise, go to this URL: https://nowsparkcreativity.com/2020/02/how-to-use-i-am-from-poems-in-class.html.

Step 2 – When running meetings with cross-sections or your entire extended team, set up meeting rules. You can use the ones I share here or come up with your own. Just make sure that you provide a structure that guides open expression without stifling your participants' creativity.

Step 3 – Teach these techniques by example and direction to each of your team leaders so that they can build super-teams too.

In a world of constant disruption and change, highly organized super teams will give your company and DEI efforts a decided advantage.

The Time to Put These Tips to Work is Now!

In my work with hundreds of CDOs over the past post-pandemic period, I've been told that their jobs have become like sitting in the center of a storm that is not letting up. As many futurists aptly predict, the storm is gaining power and speed. Based on my research, CDOs would do well to adopt the Navy Seal motto that states, "The only easy day was yesterday." Likewise, the easiest day a CDO ever had was likely sometime in their past. We need to accept the reality that it will get more complex and disruptive from here on forward.

With all this in mind, I urge you not to wait to put these tips to work. You may think you are too busy to do it today, but you will only get even busier tomorrow. However, by putting these tips to work, you will create the organizational power needed to enable you to rise from under this burgeoning weight and begin to regain some of your balance. A balance you will need to face the new opportunities and challenges of the short and long-term future.

Bibliography

1. Chief diversity officer. s.l. : Wikipedia, 2021. https://en.wikipedia.org/wiki/Chief_diversity_officer.
2. Kulp, Tim. s.l. : HR Executive, 2021. https://hrexecutive.com/ai-and-hiring-bias-why-you-need-to-teach-your-robots-well/.
3. Bishop, Kate. Your Next Job Interview May Be with a Robot—Whether You Realize it or Not. s.l. : Observer, 2021. https://observer.com/2021/03/artificial-intelligence-job-interview-problems-bias-tips/.
4. Jovanovic, Bojan. 55 Fascinating AI Statistics and Trends for 2021. s.l. : DataProt, 2021. https://dataprot.net/statistics/ai-statistics/
5. Thomas, R Roosevelt, and Woodruff, Marjorie I. Building a House for Diversity. s.l. : AMACOM, 1999. https://www.amazon.com/Building-House-Diversity-Strategies-\
6. Bopaiah, Minal. Equity: How to Design Organizations Where Everyone Thrives. s.l. : Berrett-Koehler Publishers, 2021. https://www.amazon.com/Equity-Design-Organizations-Everyone-Thrives/dp/B09C6PPP9R/ref=sr_1_1?crid=2G0JHR3QI4CJQ&keywords=minal+bopaiah+equity&qid=1639240947&sprefix=Minal+Bopa%2Caps%2C150&sr=8-1.
7. Perez, Nereida. How Executive Sponsors Can Support Disability ERGs/BRGs. s.l. : Disability: In North Carolina, 2017. https://di-nc.org/how-executive-sponsors-can-support-disability-ergsbrgs/
8. Santana, Joseph. Supercharge Your ERGs: 18 Tips to Power-Up Your ERG/BRG Strategy. s.l. : Joseph Santana, LLC, 2018. https://www.amazon.com/Supercharge-Your-ERGs-Power-Up-Strategy/dp/1718161824/ref=tmm_pap_swatch_0?_encoding=UTF8&qid=1639257064&sr=8-1.

9. Schneider, Michael. Google Spent 2 Years Studying 180 Teams. The Most Successful Ones Shared These 5 Traits. s.l. : Inc. https://www.inc.com/michael-schneider/google-thought-they-knew-how-to-create-the-perfect.html.
10. Rozovsky, Julia. The five keys to a successful Google team. s.l. : Re: Work, 2015. https://rework.withgoogle.com/blog/five-keys-to-a-successful-google-team/.
11. Gehlback, Hunter, et al. Creating Birds of Similar Feathers: Leveraging Similarity to Improve Teacher-Student Relationships and Academic Achievement. s.l. : Journal of Educational Psychology, 2016. https://www.apa.org/pubs/journals/features/edu-0000042.pdf.

PART III

The Future of DEI Belongs to Leaders Who Are MacGyver's

MacGyver is the title character and name of an American TV series. Back in 1985, he was played by Richard Dean Anderson. Most recently, actor Lucas Till played the role in a 2016 reboot. In the program, MacGyver is a genius who improvises ways to make new solutions and get out of impossible situations using whatever items he finds at hand. The show and concept were so popular that the term "to Macgyver" has come to describe the act of coming up with quick and effective solutions, using whatever is available.

The ability "to Macgyver" also aptly describes a critical skill needed by today and tomorrow's DEI leaders. Why and how, is the topic of our last and final chapter in this section of this book.

CHAPTER 7

The Future Belongs to Leaders Who Are Ready for Everything

*"I can't change the direction of the wind, but I can adjust my sails to always reach my destination."–**Jimmy Dean***

As I write this final chapter, the news I'm getting is full of conflicting stories. St. Kitts, where I'll be heading in a few weeks, has lifted many of their travel restrictions. Meanwhile, Cornell University canceled a ceremony for December graduates, closed libraries, and took other restrictive measures on Tuesday, December 14, 2021, after the school's coronavirus testing lab found evidence of the Omicron variant in several students' test specimens. Final exams scheduled for this week have been switched to an online format. Fitness centers and gyms were closed, and athletic events were canceled. In an article in VOX by Umair Irfan, published December 15, 2021, we see the bold sub-headline. "Omicron may be less risky for each of us — but riskier for all of us." According to the article, the silver lining is that Omicron is less deadly than other variants. The cloud is that Omicron is far more contagious. And these announcements pretty much capture the rhythm of our news. We are constantly tossed from a state of "yikes, are we headed back to massive shutdowns and stay-home orders, to the old freedoms are coming back!" Hearing shifting news like this, makes people groan with mental whiplash.

"When will things stabilize?" some may wonder "When will life return to some semblance of what it used to be so we can get on with our lives?" question others. The belief is that if only things would settle down, we can go back to planning the way we used to plan, and all will be good.

But the fact is that the belief that things were ever stable and predictable was only an illusion. The potential outcomes may have been fewer extreme opposites, but they've always been unpredictable. This story about a wise ancient farmer told by the Chinese philosopher, Lao Tzu, who lived in the sixth century B.C., illustrates this point. Here is my abridged version of the story.

One day, an emperor with a large army camped near a village. When the emperor saw a horse that belonged to a farmer, he instantly fell in love with it. He sent his people to offer the farmer whatever he wanted for the horse. "Oh, how lucky you are; the emperor wants to buy your horse," said all the farmer's neighbors. But the farmer replied, "Who knows." When the farmer refused to sell his beloved horse to the emperor, all his neighbors said, "What have you done? Now the emperor will take the horse by force and punish you. This will bring bad luck to you and your family." But the farmer replied, "Who knows." The next day the horse went missing, and the neighbors assumed that the emperor's people had stolen it. "What bad luck," they said to the farmer. "You did not want to sell the horse to the emperor, and now he took it, and you are left with nothing." Once again, the farmer stoically replied, "Maybe yes, maybe no. Who knows?" The following day, the horse came running back and brought seven strong wild horses. The neighbors gathered around the farmer and expressed their delight. "This is just wonderful. How fortunate you were not to sell the horse. Now you have eight beautiful, strong horses instead of just one." The farmer relaxed, calmly shrugged his shoulders, and replied, "Fortunate or unfortunate. Who knows?" The farmer's son, who helped his elderly father with the work on the farm, started taming the wild horses right away. But a mare threw him over. And as a result, he fell and broke his right leg. Due to the accident, the son would remain bedridden for months and could not help his father with the farm. The neighbors were quick to say to the farmer, "Oh, this is awful. Such bad luck." The farmer helping his son with his injury replied softly, "Good luck, or bad luck. Who can say, who knows?" A few weeks later, a war broke out. The army came to the village and forced all able-bodied men to join the military and fight the invaders. However, due to his broken leg, the farmer's son was left at home with his father. The neighbors were devastated that their sons were sent off to the front and, not knowing whether they would ever see them again, said to the farmer, "How lucky, your son is safe." Again, the farmer replied, "Good luck or bad luck. How do we know?"

The moral of the story is simple. We historically label things as good omens or bad omens because we think different events indicate good or bad tidings for what is ultimately an unknown future. For many people today, a good omen means an opportunity is appearing that they can seize, while a bad omen means they should hunker down and wait for the storm to pass. But unfortunately, in today's world of regular rollercoaster disruptions, we would be in a constant state of "fits and starts" if we continue to follow that pattern. To succeed in this world of disruption, we need a new approach. We need to run our DEI operations rooted around the philosophy captured in the American Novelist, Tom Robbins quote. "A truly stable system expects the unexpected, is prepared to be disrupted, waits to be transformed." In summary, we need always to be ready to make the most of every single transformative disruption.

In his famous last lecture, Randy Pausch, a Carnegie Mellon University computer scientist with terminal pancreatic cancer, brought this point home better than anyone during his last days. In that speech, Pausch aptly stated, "We cannot change the cards we are dealt, just how we play the hand." One anonymous writer in Quora estimates that two-thirds of the cards held by a poker player during a game will be flops. Yet good players win between ninety in low stake games and sixty percent in higher stake games. How? By the way, they play their cards.

The world is full of success stories that happened during what most of us would consider the worst of circumstances, equivalent to being dealt a bad hand. I'm particularly fond of one story my mother told me when I was a child. It's one of those stories a parent tells their kids to convey a point, and you wonder later if it were true or fictitious. It's the story of someone who maximized his opportunities during the height of the Great Depression, while others waited for the good times to return. This story, like the earlier one, is also about a farmer. In this case, a young farmer with a wife, two children, and very little money. As he looked at all the other tiny houses near him, he noticed how people would make a long daily trek into quarry areas to buy expensive coal chips they used for cooking and heating. He only had a few dollars and didn't own a wagon, so he borrowed money and a wagon from his uncle. Early in the morning, he went to the quarry and bought a large chunk of coal at wholesale and a sheet of burlap. Out of the burlap, he made little pouches. Next, he chopped up the big piece of coal into chips he could fit into the small bags. Finally, the young farmer got on his wagon and rode from house to house, selling the pouches of coal at a competitive price and eliminating his neighbor's long treks. With his profits, he paid his uncle for the loan and rental of the wagon, plus had enough to feed his family and buy another chunk of coal. Thus, he thrived during the depression and gradually built a family fuel delivery business that later brought propane and serviced in-home equipment. Meanwhile, as my mother pointed out, others that waited for the depression to end so they could resume their lives didn't fare half as well.

As a futurist DEI leader, I advise you not to scan the future looking for what you deem a good opportunity to act or a bad one to avoid. I believe you should ask yourself, "What are the potential outcomes of any trends I'm seeing take shape, and how can I drive the maximum benefit to my workforce, workplace, and marketplace, regardless of which situation materializes?" Like the baseball hitter we spoke about back in chapter three, you want to be ready to take the best action regardless of what type of ball the pitcher sends your way. You want to be the embodiment of that "truly stable system" that "expects the unexpected, is prepared to be disrupted," and "waits to be transformed."

The key ingredients behind the baseball player's success, as noted earlier, are superior vision and a system tuned to react most appropriately to any situation. The focus of this book has been to give you the equivalent of those two ingredients—one, the future foresight tools you need to see the trends that are taking shape. And two, several tips you as an ERG or DEI leader can follow to prepare to respond to whatever situation you see coming your way rapidly. Taken together, these two elements prepare you to deal with anything the future throws your way. But to win, you have to play. You need to avoid the tendency to wait for a better opportunity.

In his book, *Illusions,* the American author Richard Bach aptly stated that "What the caterpillar calls the end of the world, the master calls a butterfly." There are many interpretations of this cryptic quote. The one I like best is this one. What the caterpillar sees as an end to its life as it spins and enters the cocoon that marks the end of life as it has known it is actually the beginning of a new life known only to the master who possesses greater wisdom. I trust that armed with these 21st-century tools, you will become a "master, who can turn any situation, even one that to too many may seem catastrophic, to your advantage.

In closing, I would like to leave you with some insightful and powerful words from a speech by the 44th President of the United States, Barack Obama, to his supporters in Illinois, on February 5th, 2008. "Change will not come if we wait for some other person or if we wait for some other time. We are the ones we've been waiting for." And to that, I will add this is time to act. This is the time to take our efforts to the next historic level. Welcome to a world of new and infinite possibilities for a more diverse, equitable, and inclusive future!

Acknowledgments

In closing, I would like to thank the members of the CDO PowerCircle whose stories and practices provided many insights for this book. I am fortunate and blessed to be surrounded by many insightful and caring leaders.

A very special thanks to Catherine A. Jacobson, President and CEO of Froedtert Health, for taking the time in the middle of a continuing pandemic to provide her Foreword to this book. Cathy's leadership of her company's DEI efforts is a role model I often recommend.

My thanks also go to the team at Word-2-Kindle, who fashioned this book out of my manuscript, and to Nauman at Professional Audiobook Editing and Mastering for creating the Audible version of this book.

Finally, I give special thanks to two ladies who profoundly shaped many of my perspectives, my wife Eileen and my mother, Irene Torres-Laing. As she has with every article and book I've ever written, Eileen read and re-read every word of this book and provided her critique and questions. Because of her, my sometimes-vague inklings and notions have taken sharper shape and become clarified into valuable stories and tips. Eileen and I don't see everything the same way, and I believe that is what enhances both of our viewpoints. Thank you, Eileen, for your loving patience and sincere support.

As for my mother, she was an energetic, unstoppable, and unforgettable presence in my life. When I think of what she did for me, it reminds me of what Sir Isaac Newton once said. In a 1675 letter to a fellow scientist, Robert Hooke, Newton wrote, "If I have seen further, it is by standing on the shoulders of giants." I was fortunate enough to be born into the arms of a woman who was in her own right a giant. Her positive spirit, clear mind, and quiet strengths were the chisels that molded me. Her teaching method was through stories like those I shared in this book. Growing up, I admit I never realized the power of her upbringing. It was much later in life after she had long passed on, that I finally saw how much she'd shaped me. It appears that in the final analysis, like our sixteenth President Abraham Lincoln, I too can say that "All that I am or hope ever to be . . . I get from my mother." Thank you, Mom. I hope this book made you proud.

Printed in Great Britain
by Amazon

39603091R00088